● COMPLETE
mince
COOKBOOK

COMPLETE

mince

COOKBOOK

BRIDGET JONES

HAMLYN

For Neill —
to extend his repertoire
of mince dishes beyond
Cottage pie and Spaghetti bolognaise.

Photography by Chris Crofton
Illustrations by Sue Lines

This edition first published in 1992
by Hamlyn, an imprint of Reed Consumer Books Limited
Michelin House, 81 Fulham Road, London SW36RB
and Auckland, Melbourne, Singapore and Toronto

Reprinted 1992

A CIP catalogue record for this book is available
from the British Library

ISBN 0 600 57584 5

Produced by Mandarin Offset
Printed and bound in China

CONTENTS

USEFUL FACTS AND FIGURES

Notes on metrication
In this book quantities are given in metric and Imperial measures. Exact conversion from Imperial to metric measures does not usually give very convenient working quantities and so the metric measures have been rounded off into units of 25 grams. The table below shows the recommended equivalents.

Ounces	Approx g to nearest whole figure	Recommended conversion to nearest unit of 25
1	28	25
2	57	50
3	85	75
4	113	100
5	142	150
6	170	175
7	198	200
8	227	225
9	255	250
10	283	275
11	312	300
12	340	350
13	368	375
14	396	400
15	425	425
16 (1 lb)	454	450
17	482	475
18	510	500
19	539	550
20 ($1\frac{1}{4}$ lb)	567	575

Note: When converting quantities over 20 oz first add the appropriate figures in the centre column, then adjust to the nearest unit of 25. As a general guide, 1 kg (1000 g) equals 2.2 lb or about 2 lb 3 oz. This method of conversion gives good results in nearly all cases, although in certain pastry and cake recipes a more accurate conversion is necessary to produce a balanced recipe.

Liquid measures The millilitre has been used in this book and the following table gives a few examples.

Imperial	Approx ml to nearest whole figure	Recommended ml
$\frac{1}{4}$ pint	142	150 ml
$\frac{1}{2}$ pint	283	300 ml
$\frac{3}{4}$ pint	425	450 ml
1 pint	567	600 ml
$1\frac{1}{2}$ pints	851	900 ml
$1\frac{3}{4}$ pints	992	1000 ml (1 litre)

Spoon measures All spoon measures given in this book are level unless otherwise stated.
Can sizes At present, cans are marked with the exact (usually to the nearest whole number) metric equivalent of the Imperial weight of the contents, so we have followed this practice when giving can sizes.

Oven temperatures

The table below gives recommended equivalents.

	°C	°F	Gas Mark
Very cool	110	225	$\frac{1}{4}$
	120	250	$\frac{1}{2}$
Cool	140	275	1
	150	300	2
Moderate	160	325	3
	180	350	4
Moderately	190	375	5
hot	200	400	6
Hot	220	425	7
	230	450	8
Very hot	240	475	9

Notes for American and Australian users

In America the 8-fl oz measuring cup is used. In Australia metric measures are now used in conjunction with the standard 250-ml measuring cup. The Imperial pint, used in Britain and Australia, is 20 fl oz, while the American pint is 16 fl oz. It is important to remember that the Australian tablespoon differs from both the British and American tablespoons; the table below gives a comparison. The British standard tablespoon, which has been used throughout this book, holds 17.7 ml, the American 14.2 ml, and the Australian 20 ml. A teaspoon holds approximately 5 ml in all three countries.

British	American	Australian	
1	1	1	teaspoon
1	1	1	tablespoon
2	3	2	tablespoons
$3\frac{1}{2}$	4	3	tablespoons
4	5	$3\frac{1}{2}$	tablespoons

An Imperial/American guide to solid and liquid measures

Solid measures

Imperial	American
1 lb butter or margarine	2 cups
1 lb flour	4 cups
1 lb granulated or caster sugar	2 cups
1 lb icing sugar	3 cups
8 oz rice	1 cup

Liquid measures

Imperial	American
$\frac{1}{4}$ pint liquid	$\frac{2}{3}$ cup liquid
$\frac{1}{2}$ pint	$1\frac{1}{4}$ cups
$\frac{3}{4}$ pint	2 cups
1 pint	$2\frac{1}{2}$ cups
$1\frac{1}{2}$ pints	$3\frac{3}{4}$ cups
2 pints	5 cups ($2\frac{1}{2}$ pints)

NOTE: WHEN MAKING ANY OF THE RECIPES IN THIS BOOK, ONLY FOLLOW ONE SET OF MEASURES AS THEY ARE NOT INTERCHANGEABLE.

INTRODUCTION

Mince is one of those foods which was looked upon for many years as a very cheap necessity for mid-week family meals, but it was always abandoned for better things the minute the purse would allow. This is not really surprising, as it is fair to say that many old-fashioned British mince dishes were indescribably dull.

So whatever happened to improve the status of mince? Perhaps it is a consequence of foreign travel and the wider availability of spices and unusual ingredients from all over the world, but whatever the reasons, mince is now used in all sorts of far from dull recipes. Beef, pork, lamb and veal are all available as mince to make an exciting range of dishes from the economical to the exotic. Heart-warming, homely cottage pie is a sure winner for family suppers; mouth-watering moussaka often revives happy memories of holiday meals, and that firm appetite-raiser, lasagne, almost cannot fail to please. This is all evidence that mince is no longer the depressed offering of a poor cook but is now recognised for its true culinary worth.

However, the real value of minced meat for any dish depends entirely on its quality, a point which must be emphasised. Coarse fatty minced meat will not produce good results, so look out for lean, finely minced, good-quality meat. If you have a good butcher or live near a reliable supermarket then you are unlikely to have problems but if you have doubts about the quality of the mince you are buying, the following guidelines may be helpful.

Minced beef or lamb should be quite rich and bright in colour, not pale red or pink. If the meat looks pale then it probably has a high fat content. Look out for fine, moist mince and minced steak because it is superior to minced beef. Avoid any mince which looks dry and dark brown in colour. You can always ask a butcher if he will mince some meat especially for you – most will be quite happy to do this given that you order the meat in advance. Many supermarkets with butchers on the premises will also oblige by mincing meat if you are buying more

than just a pound or so. Alternatively, put chunks of meat through a mincer or food processor yourself if you have the time.

Shoulder of lamb, trimmed of skin and excess fat, yields excellent lean mince and it is very important that minced lamb is as lean as possible. Shoulder or spare rib pork can be trimmed and minced successfully; lean stewing steak, chuck steak or even rump and fillet steak can be used, depending on the recipe. Pie veal is the cheapest cut to use if you cannot find ready minced veal.

Minced turkey and chicken are used in some dishes. Boneless chicken breasts or part-boned joints are the easiest to mince but for economy skin and bone a whole chicken, then mince the meat. Again you may be lucky enough to know a good butcher who will do this for you. Boneless turkey is available in many forms: as breast fillets or shaped into roasting joints, both of which can be minced. I am lucky in that I have found a good local butcher who prepared pounds and pounds of minced meats for me when I tested the recipes for this book. For this and for a prompt and friendly delivery service, I really owe a big 'thank you' to B & M Tooley of Guildford.

The recipes in this book will offer ideas for every occasion, from cheap and cheerful dishes for when you are a little short of cash to exciting dishes to serve at dinner parties. You will probably notice that I have used freshly ground black pepper all the way through. That's because I really do find that it gives the best flavour, but you can use whichever seasoning you prefer.

I can truthfully say that although I sometimes had to test as many as ten recipes a day for this book, not once did we lose appetite for the food – and that must be the highest recommendation for the exceptional versatility of good old mince!

Bridget Jones

CANAPÉS AND FIRST COURSES

For the opening course of a meal, mince is unlikely to rival the simplicity of the avocado pear or the instant elegance of the ogen melon for speed and ease, but if offers a number of first-course options many of which are both original and delicious.

Wun Tun Soup

Wun tuns are small Chinese dumplings consisting of a thin wrapping of dough with a small amount of filling. Here they are filled with minced pork and each one encloses a prawn. The dumplings are cooked in a light chicken soup to make a moderately filling first course. If you live near a Chinese supermarket then you can buy the wun tun wrappers.

Dough
50 g/2 oz plain flour
50 g/2 oz cornflour
salt and freshly ground black
　pepper
2 eggs, beaten separately
2 tablespoons water
Filling
100 g/4 oz minced pork
a few drops of sesame oil
1 tablespoon soy sauce

2 tablespoons chopped spring
　onion
18 peeled cooked prawns
Soup
25 g/1 oz butter
1 chicken joint
1 onion, peeled and chopped
bay leaf
1 chicken stock cube
900 ml/1½ pints water

To make the dough, sift the flour and cornflour into a bowl and add a pinch of salt. Make a well in the middle. Beat one egg with the water, then pour this into the well and work in the dry ingredients to make a firm dough. Turn the dough on to a floured surface and knead until smooth, then wrap it in cling film and set it aside.

　For the filling mix the pork with the sesame oil and the soy sauce. Mix the spring onions into the meat. Take a prawn, then knead a little of the meat mixture around it to make a small meatball with the prawn completely enclosed. Repeat with the remaining prawns and meat.

　Now make the soup. Melt the butter in a saucepan. Add the chicken joint and the onion and cook until the joint is lightly browned and the onion is soft. Put the bay leaf in the pan and crumble in the stock cube then pour in the water and bring to the boil. Reduce the heat, cover the pan and simmer for 30 minutes. Lift the chicken out of the soup, cut the meat off it, shred it and return it to the soup, discarding the bones.

To make the wun tuns, divide the dough in half. Take one portion and roll it out into a square measuring 25 cm/10 in. Cut this into nine small squares. Take each one in turn and roll it out again so that the dough is as thin as you dare make it. Place one of the prawn-filled meatballs on the dough and brush the edge with beaten egg. Fold the dough around the meatball and gather it together like a little bag, with the edges of the dough free. Make sure the filling is well sealed in. Set the wun tun aside on a well floured plate and repeat the process.

Cook the wun tuns in the simmering soup for 5 minutes, then serve piping hot. **Serves 4**

Lemon Soup with Spiced Lamb Meatballs

Rich, spicy lamb meatballs contrast well with a clear and tangy lemon soup. This is particularly good as the first course if you are serving a fish dish for the main course. Offer warm pitta bread with the soup.

Soup	Meatballs
1 large onion, peeled and finely chopped	225 g/8 oz minced lamb
bay leaf	50 g/2 oz fresh breadcrumbs
25 g/1 oz butter	1 clove garlic, peeled and crushed
2 chicken stock cubes	1 tablespoon ground cumin
900 ml/1½ pints water	1 small onion, peeled and grated
grated rind and juice of 1 lemon	1 egg, beaten
2 tablespoons cream sherry	2 tablespoons chopped fresh coriander leaves
salt and freshly ground black pepper	oil for deep frying

First make the soup. Fry the onion and bay leaf in the butter until soft but not browned. Crumble in the stock cubes and pour in the water. Add the lemon rind and juice, then bring to the boil, stirring all the time. Cover the pan and simmer gently for 20 minutes.

Make the meatballs while the soup is simmering. Mix the lamb with all the other ingredients and shape the mixture into 20 small walnut-sized meatballs. Heat the oil for deep frying to 180 C/350 F or until a cube of bread browns in 30 seconds. Add the meatballs and fry them very briefly. Meanwhile, taste the soup and add seasoning and the sherry. Drain the meatballs on absorbent kitchen paper and add them to the soup, then continue to simmer for 2 to 3 minutes.

Ladle the soup and meatballs into individual bowls and serve piping hot. **Serves 4**

Rich Pork Pâté

(Illustrated on page 25)

*This is a full-flavoured pâté which can be served with plenty of French
bread and a full-bodied red wine to make a satisfying lunch. If you are
offering it as the first course, then have hot toast as an accompaniment.*

450 g/1 lb pig's liver
50 g/2 oz butter
1 large onion, peeled and finely
   chopped
3 cloves garlic, peeled and
   crushed
450 g/1 lb minced pork
1 tablespoon juniper berries,
   crushed

1 teaspoon paprika
salt and freshly ground black
   pepper
6 tablespoons brandy
2 bay leaves
a few whole juniper berries to
   garnish

Chop the liver – it does not have to be too fine, but large chunks would
not be right in the finished pâté. Melt the butter in a large frying pan
and brown the liver quickly all over. It is important to make sure that
the liver is well sealed and that it is cooked quickly so that the flavour is
kept in each piece. Remove the cooked liver from the pan and place it in
a large bowl. Fry the onion and garlic very briefly to take away their
raw taste, then add them, with all the pan juices, to the liver.

Mix the minced pork and juniper berries into the liver, then add the
paprika and seasoning to taste – be fairly generous. Stir in the brandy
then mix thoroughly. Turn the mixture into an ovenproof dish – a plain
round one which holds about 900 ml/1½ pints is best. Make sure the
dish is not too full or juices could be lost during cooking. Smooth the
top then arrange the bay leaves and whole berries on top. Cover with
cooking foil, stand the dish in a roasting tin, and pour in enough boiling
water to come up to the top of the tin. Bake the pâté in a moderate oven
(160 C, 325 F, gas 3) for 2 hours.

Remove the pâté from the water bath, place a plate on top and weight
this down to press the pâté. If you do not have a plate which fits just
inside the top of the cooking dish, then use a large piece of cooking foil,
folded several times. Allow the pâté to cool then chill it overnight, still
with the weights on.

Serve the pâté straight from the dish. Any left over can be frozen for
up to 6 months but it will keep quite successfully in the refrigerator for
several days. **Serves 8 to 10**

Herb Pâté

(Illustrated on page 25)

*This is a smooth, simple pâté which makes an excellent first course. Serve
melba toast and pieces of celery stick as an accompaniment.*

450 g/1 lb minced pork
450 g/1 lb lamb's liver
1 large Spanish onion, peeled
   and very finely chopped or
   minced
3 large cloves garlic, peeled and
   crushed
2 teaspoons dried thyme

1 teaspoon rubbed sage
2 tablespoons chopped parsley
1 teaspoon ground mace
freshly grated nutmeg
salt and freshly ground black
   pepper
4 tablespoons brandy or sherry
2 large bay leaves

Put the pork in a large bowl. Mince the liver or purée it in a food
processor or liquidiser, then add it to the pork. Add the onion, stir in
the garlic, herbs and mace, add a generous sprinkling of nutmeg and
seasoning, then pour in the brandy or sherry and stir until all the
ingredients are thoroughly mixed.

Grease a 1-kg/2-lb loaf tin thoroughly and lay the bay leaves neatly
in the base. If you have any fears of the pâté sticking to the base of the
tin, then line it with an oblong of greased greaseproof paper first. Spoon
the pâté into the container, putting a couple of spoonfuls in first to keep
the bay leaves in place. Smooth the top, stand the tin in a roasting tin,
pour boiling water into the roasting tin to surround the loaf tin then
bake the pâté in a moderate oven (160 C, 325 F, gas 3) for $2\frac{1}{2}$ hours.

Cover the pâté with greased greaseproof paper or foil and place
heavy weights on top to press it. Leave it to cool, then chill it for several
hours or overnight, still with the weights on top. To serve, turn the pâté
out of the tin so that the bay leaves are on top, then cut it into slices or
serve it whole. **Serves 8 to 10**

Melba Toast

To make melba toast use sliced bread – medium-thick slices are best.
Toast the bread lightly on each side then, working quickly so that the
bread does not cool and become too crisp, cut off the crusts and slice
horizontally through each slice of toast. Put these very thin slices,
untoasted side uppermost, on a grill rack and cook them (quite far away
from the grill) until they are curled and lightly browned. Take great
care not to burn the toast at this stage. Once cooled the melba toast will
keep successfully in an airtight tin for several days.

Peppered Mushroom Pâté

The addition of red vermouth enriches the flavour of the chopped green pepper and mushrooms in this otherwise simple pâté. Serve with Granary bread or wholemeal rolls to make this a substantial starter.

450 g/1 lb lamb's liver
3 tablespoons oil
1 large onion, peeled and finely
   chopped
2 large cloves garlic, peeled and
   crushed
1 large green pepper

175 g/6 oz mushrooms
450 g/1 lb minced pork
150 ml/$\frac{1}{4}$ pint red vermouth
salt and freshly ground black
   pepper
$\frac{1}{2}$ teaspoon ground mixed spice

Finely chop the liver. Heat the oil in a large frying pan, then add the liver, onion and garlic and fry until the liver is browned all over. Stir the mixture fairly frequently to make sure that it does not stick to the pan or burn on one side.

Meanwhile, halve the pepper, remove the stalk, seeds and pith, then chop finely. This is easiest if you cut each half into fine strips then slice across them to give very small pieces. Add to the liver mixture and cook for 2 minutes.

Chop the mushrooms, then mix them in a bowl with the pork and vermouth. Add plenty of seasoning and the mixed spice, then stir in the cooked ingredients and mix thoroughly, making sure that the mince is well broken up. Transfer the pâté to a greased 1-kg/2-lb loaf tin and stand it in a roasting tin. Pour in boiling water to come almost to the top of the outer tin, then bake in a moderate oven (160 C, 325 F, gas 3) for 1$\frac{1}{2}$ hours.

Cover the pâté with greased greaseproof paper or foil and place weights on top to press it. Allow it to cool, then chill it overnight or for several hours, still with the weights in place. Serve the pâté sliced, either arranged on one platter or on individual plates. **Serves 8**

Easy chilli con carne

Comfort food at its best • Low in fat • 1 of your 5 a day

1 Heat the oil in a large non-stick sauté pan. Add the soffritto mix and garlic and cook over a low heat for 3-4 minutes until softened but not browned. Push the vegetables to the side of the pan and turn up the heat. Add the mince and break up with a wooden spoon. Cook for 3-4 minutes until lightly browned.

2 Add the oregano, chilli powder, Worcestershire sauce and tomato purée. Stir well then add the stock. Bring to the boil, half cover the pan with a lid and simmer for 25 minutes until the liquid has reduced by half.

3 Add the beans to the pan and bring to the boil. Simmer for 10 minutes then serve with baked potatoes and a fresh green salad.

1 tbsp olive oil

400g pack Cooks' Ingredients Soffritto Mix

2 cloves garlic, chopped

400g extra lean Aberdeen Angus beef mince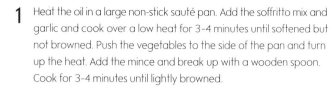

2 tbsp chopped fresh oregano

1 tsp hot chilli powder

3 tbsp **Lea & Perrins Worcestershire Sauce**

2 tbsp essential Waitrose Tomato Purée

500g tub Cooks' Ingredients Beef Stock

2 x 400g cans red kidney beans, drained and rinsed

Small baked potatoes and crisp green salad, to serve

Cook's tips

Try spooning the chilli into taco shells filled with shredded lettuce and serve topped with some chopped avocado.

This dish is great for freezing – spoon into a suitable container and freeze for up to 3 months. Defrost thoroughly and reheat until piping hot before serving.

You can comment on this recipe and thousands more by visiting our website. Join the debate at Waitrose.com

Nutrition 431kcals/29.2g protein/58.4g carbohydrate/9g sugars/ 8.9g fat/2.9g saturated fat/9.5g fibre/0.6g salt per serving

PEFC Certified

This product is from sustainably managed forests and controlled sources

PEFC™

www.pefc.org

Some products are available only in larger branches. Subject to availability. Excludes Little Waitrose and concessions. Waitrose Limited, Bracknell, Berkshire, RG12 8YA. Find great offers in branch and at Waitrose.com.

Championing British
The Waitrose way

January 2013

Philadelphia Meatballs

(Illustrated on page 28)

These meatballs can be made, shaped and coated with egg and breadcrumbs well in advance ready for deep frying at the last minute. As well as making a good starter, they can be skewered on to small wooden cocktail sticks and served with drinks.

450 g/1 lb minced beef
1 teaspoon anchovy essence
2 tablespoons chopped parsley
generous dash of Worcestershire
    sauce
freshly ground black pepper
225 g/8 oz Philadelphia cheese
flour for coating

1 egg, beaten
100–175 g/4–6 oz fine dry
    breadcrumbs
oil for deep frying
Garnish
1 lettuce heart, shredded
sprigs of watercress
4 wedges of lemon

Mix the beef with the anchovy essence, parsley, Worcestershire sauce and pepper to taste, making sure all the ingredients are thoroughly combined. Divide the Philadelphia cheese into 16 small portions and do the same with the meat mixture. Flatten a portion of the meat on the palm of your hand, place a portion of the cheese in the middle then fold the meat around it to enclose it completely. Roll the meatball in your hand to make sure the meat is bound together. Repeat the process with the remaining meat and cheese.

Coat the meatballs first in the flour, then in the beaten egg and finally in the breadcrumbs, pressing them on well. Chill the coated meatballs thoroughly to give the coating time to set.

Heat the oil to 180 C/350 F or until a cube of bread browns in 30 seconds then add several meatballs and cook until they are golden brown and crisp. Drain on absorbent kitchen paper and keep hot until all the meatballs are cooked.

To serve, arrange the lettuce on four small individual plates. Pile the meatballs on the plates, then garnish with the watercress and add a wedge of lemon to each plate. The juice from the lemon is squeezed over the meatballs just before they are eaten. **Serves 4**

Beef Canapés

(Illustrated on pages 26/27)

These delicious savoury snacks can be prepared quite far in advance ready for grilling at the last minute. There are dozens of ways in which the canapés can be served, and some suggestions for varying the basic recipe are given below. As well as making a good alternative to a formal first course, they can be prepared in large numbers for parties – why not try cooking them on a barbecue?

450 g/1 lb minced steak
4 teaspoons prepared mustard
  (for example, horseradish
  mustard, French mustard or
  wholegrain mustard)
1 clove garlic, peeled and
  crushed
4 teaspoons chopped chives

salt and freshly ground black
  pepper
16 high-baked water biscuits or
  toast circles to serve
Garnish
100 g/4 oz Philadelphia cheese
8 stuffed green olives

Place the minced steak in a bowl, then mix in the mustard, garlic and chives and season to taste, mixing thoroughly to make sure the ingredients are well combined. Spread the mixture evenly over the biscuits or circles of toast right up to the edges to prevent the bases from overcooking, then place them under a hot grill and cook until the meat is browned.

Meanwhile, cut the cheese into 16 small neat cubes and cut the olives in half. Top each of the canapés with a piece of cheese and an olive half and serve at once. **Makes 16**

Different Toppings

Chilli Beef Canapés. Omit the mustard from the above recipe and stir in chilli powder to taste instead. Add about 2 teaspoons ground cumin to the mixture then cook the canapés as above. Top them with mashed avocado pear and a wedge of tomato.

Beef and Mushroom Canapés. Wipe 16 small button mushrooms and press one into the middle of each portion of beef, then grill as in the main recipe. Garnish each one with a parsley sprig and serve.

Curried Beef Canapés. Omit the mustard from the main recipe and stir in a tablespoon garam masala (available in cans or packets from good supermarkets, delicatessens or oriental shops). Cook the canapés as above, then top each one with a slice of cucumber and a sprig of fresh coriander.

Beef and Oyster Canapés. Add the grated rind of $\frac{1}{2}$ lemon to the meat mixture. Cook the canapés as in the main recipe. Top each one with a little mayonnaise and a couple of canned smoked oysters (available quite cheaply from some supermarkets and delicatessens). Serve at once.

Veal and Roquefort Croquettes

(Illustrated on pages 26/27)

If you wish you can double up on the quantities for these croquettes and serve them as a main dish. If you decide to do that, then serve a hot sauce made from Béchamel Sauce (see page 162) with the chopped eggs stirred in. Pork can be substituted for the veal in this recipe.

225 g/8 oz minced veal
50 g/2 oz fresh breadcrumbs
1 small egg, beaten
salt and freshly ground black
   pepper
2 tablespoons chopped chives
100 g/4 oz Roquefort cheese
Coating
plain flour
1 egg, beaten
50 g/2 oz fine dry breadcrumbs

Sauce
2 hard-boiled eggs
150 ml/$\frac{1}{4}$ pint mayonnaise
4 tablespoons single cream
dash of lemon juice
garlic salt
oil for deep frying
Garnish
1 head of radiccio
1 lemon, cut into 8 wedges

Mix the veal with the breadcrumbs, beaten egg, seasoning and chives. Make sure all the ingredients are thoroughly combined, then divide the mixture into four equal portions. Cut the Roquefort into four equal fingers about 5 cm/2 in long.

Take each portion of the meat mixture and shape it into a small neat roll around one of the pieces of cheese. Coat the rolls first in a little flour, then in the beaten egg and finally in the breadcrumbs, making sure the meat is completely covered in breadcrumbs. Chill the croquettes for several hours or put them in the freezer for a while, until the coating is hard.

For the sauce, press the hard-boiled eggs through a sieve, then mix them with the mayonnaise and cream. Stir in the lemon juice and add garlic salt to taste. Chill this sauce thoroughly until you are ready to serve the croquettes.

Heat the oil for deep frying to 180 C/350 F or until a cube of bread browns in 30 seconds. Add the croquettes and cook until golden then drain on absorbent kitchen paper. To serve, arrange the radiccio leaves on individual plates and put one croquette on each. Add the lemon wedges and pour just a little of the sauce over each croquette. Serve the remaining sauce separately. **Serves 4**

Note: radiccio is a type of Italian chicory which is red in colour and which resembles a lettuce heart in size and shape. If this vegetable is not available, then a lettuce heart can be used instead.

Stuffed Pitta Bread with Sesame Yogurt Sauce

(Illustrated on pages 26/27)

The pieces of stuffed pitta bread can be filled well in advance, wrapped in cooking foil and chilled ready for cooking just before the meal is served. The uncooked pitta bread can also be frozen to make a useful standby for a quick light meal.

225 g/8 oz minced lamb
1 small onion, peeled and very
   finely chopped
1 tablespoon chopped fresh
   mint
1 teaspoon ground cumin
salt and freshly ground black
   pepper
2 pieces pitta bread

Sesame yogurt sauce
4 tablespoons tahini
1 clove garlic, peeled and
   crushed
150 ml/$\frac{1}{4}$ pint natural yogurt
Garnish
$\frac{1}{2}$ cucumber
1 medium carrot
piece fresh root ginger (optional)

Mix the lamb with the onion and mint, then stir in the cumin and seasoning to taste. When all the ingredients are thoroughly combined roughly divide the mixture into quarters. Lay the pieces of pitta bread flat on a board, cut them in half and carefully insert a knife into each half to open the 'pocket'. Take each portion of the meat mixture in turn, knead it well together then press it into one of the pitta pockets. Make sure the meat is evenly distributed in the bread, then flatten the pitta neatly. Wrap each one in a piece of cooking foil, place on a baking tray and cook in a moderately hot oven (200 C, 400 F, gas 6) for 30 minutes.

While the bread is cooking mix together the ingredients for the sauce and leave to chill it until you are ready to serve. For the garnish, cut the cucumber, first in half lengthways, then across into pieces about the length of your finger. Cut these into fine strips. Trim the carrot and cut it in half lengthways, then into strips similar to the cucumber. Peel the ginger (if used), slice it thinly and cut the slices into fine strips. Mix all the ingredients together.

Remove the bread from the oven and cut each piece in half down the middle. Arrange the pieces on a warmed serving platter, overlapping them in a herringbone fashion, sprinkle the garnish down the middle and serve at once. Alternatively arrange the pitta on individual plates and hand the sauce separately. **Serves 4**

Notes: The quantities given here are fairly small to allow for the fact that a main course will follow. If you like, double the quantities of the meat filling and pitta. The sauce and garnishing ingredients can remain the same. Tahini is a paste made from sesame seeds, available in health food shops, delicatessens and Greek shops.

Stuffed Mushrooms

*These are quick and easy to prepare in advance, ready for speedy last-
minute cooking just before dinner. Serve with bread and butter as a starter,
or alternatively, double the quantities and serve as a light main dish.*

1 quantity Walnut and Caper
  Cheese (page 171)
4 large open mushrooms
225 g/8 oz minced pork
2 teaspoons marjoram
1 clove garlic, peeled and
  crushed

salt and freshly ground black
  pepper
2 tablespoons sesame seeds
4 lettuce leaves to serve

Prepare the flavoured cream cheese according to the recipe
instructions. Cut the stalks off the mushrooms and wipe the caps. Mix
the pork with the marjoram, garlic and seasoning to taste, then use your
hands to knead the mixture together. Divide the meat into four, shape
each portion into a small cake about the same size as the mushrooms,
and place in the mushroom caps, pressing firmly but gently and making
sure the meat comes well up to the edge of each mushroom. Sprinkle the
sesame seeds on top. Place the stuffed mushrooms in a greased
ovenproof dish and cook in a hot oven (220 C, 425 F, gas 7) for 30
minutes.

Cut four slices off the cream cheese and place one on each of the
cooked mushrooms. Serve the mushrooms, each placed in a lettuce leaf,
on individual plates. **Serves 4**

For a Main Course
Meaty stuffed mushrooms can also be served as the main course of the
meal. Double the quantities in the above recipe and continue to cook
the mushrooms in the same way.

Alternatively, press the meat filling well into the mushrooms, then
coat them completely in a little seasoned flour, beaten egg and plenty of
dry white breadcrumbs. Chill the stuffed mushrooms for about 20
minutes, then deep fry them until golden and cooked through. Drain on
absorbent kitchen paper and serve freshly cooked, with a Rich Tomato
Sauce (page 163).

Savoury Doughnuts

These slightly unusual savouries make a good first course to serve if the main dish is fairly light. It is important to add attractive garnishing ingredients so as to make the doughnuts look more interesting.

3 teaspoons dried yeast
1 teaspoon sugar
150 ml/¼ pint lukewarm water
225 g/8 oz strong white flour
1 teaspoon salt
2 teaspoons marjoram
Filling
2 tablespoons oil
1 small onion, peeled and finely chopped
1 large clove garlic, peeled and crushed
450 g/1 lb minced beef

2 teaspoons horseradish mustard or other strong mustard
100 g/4 oz matured Cheddar cheese
salt and freshly ground black pepper
8 button mushrooms
Rich Tomato Sauce (page 163) to serve
oil for deep frying
Garnish
1 small onion
1 medium carrot

First prepare the dough: sprinkle the yeast and sugar over the water and leave it in a warm place for about 15 to 20 minutes, or until the yeast has dissolved and the liquid is frothy. Sift the flour and salt into a bowl and add the marjoram. Give the yeast liquid a good stir, then make a well in the centre of the dry ingredients, pour in the liquid and gradually mix the flour into it to form a dough. Turn out on to a floured surface and knead thoroughly for about 10 minutes or until smooth then place in a lightly oiled bowl, cover with cling film or a dampened tea-towel and leave in a warm place until doubled in size. The rising time depends on the surrounding temperature, but if the dough is left in a very warm room it should be well risen in 30 to 40 minutes. If the room temperature is not high enough, the dough can be risen in a warm grill compartment of the cooker (but make certain that it is not too hot and that the heat is turned off), in an airing cupboard or near a radiator.

Meanwhile prepare the filling: heat the oil in a frying pan and add the onion and garlic. Cook, stirring frequently, until the onion is soft but not browned. Add the mince and fry it, breaking it up with a wooden spoon, until browned. Stir in the mustard, remove the pan from the heat, allow the mixture to cool slightly, then stir in the cheese and add seasoning to taste. Wipe the mushrooms and trim off the ends of their stalks. Roughly divide the meat mixture into eight portions. Take each one in turn in your hand, lightly knead the meat together and flatten it to form a thick cake. Place a mushroom in the middle and knead the mixture around it to form a meatball.

When the dough has risen, turn it out on to a floured surface and lightly knead it. Shape it into a cylinder and cut this into eight equal portions. Roll each one in turn into a circle, place one of the meatballs on top and gently work the dough around the meatball, pinching the edges together to seal in the filling. The dough should cover the meat thinly but evenly. Put the doughnuts on a greased baking tray and cover them with a piece of oiled cling film or polythene. Set aside in a warm place until the dough has doubled in size.

Prepare the sauce following the recipe instructions. For the garnish, slice the onion and separate the slices into rings. Cut the carrot in half, then cut it lengthways into thin slices and cut these into fine strips.

Heat the oil for deep frying to 180 C/350 F or until a cube of bread browns in 30 seconds. Carefully slide the doughnuts on to a draining spoon and lower them one by one into the oil. Fry, turning once, until golden brown. (You may have to use a slotted spoon to hold the doughnuts in the oil if you find them bobbing over on to the same side all the time.) Drain on absorbent kitchen paper and serve at once. Arrange the onion rings and fine strips of carrot next to the doughnuts on individual plates then serve with the tomato sauce. **Makes 8**

Savoury Scotch Doughnuts

If you like, prepare savoury doughnuts filled with a pork mixture, which has been wrapped around hard-boiled eggs. Make the dough as in the main recipe but using double the quantities: this is to allow for the fact that the meatball filling will be larger. Use minced pork instead of the minced beef and omit the mushrooms, instead wrap the meat mixture around 8 hard-boiled eggs. Enclose these completely in the dough and cook as in the main recipe. These are particularly good for taking on picnics or for serving cut in half with salad for a light main course.

Stuffed Tomatoes with Soured Cream Sauce

Minced lamb or beef can be substituted for the pork which is used to fill these tomatoes. Serve warm crusty bread or French bread to accompany them.

4 beef tomatoes
1 small onion, peeled and finely chopped
350 g/12 oz minced pork
40 g/1½ oz rolled oats
1 clove garlic, peeled and crushed
½ teaspoon rubbed sage
2 tablespoons tahini

salt and freshly ground black pepper
watercress sprigs to garnish
Soured Cream Sauce
150 ml/¼ pint soured cream
1 tablespoon chopped chives
a little grated nutmeg
25 g/1 oz flaked almonds, lightly toasted

Cut the tops off the tomatoes, then scoop out and discard the seeds from inside. Turn the tomato shells upside down on a double thickness of absorbent kitchen paper to drain thoroughly then mop the inside of each one with a small pad of absorbent paper.

Mix the onion with the pork, oats, garlic, sage and tahini, add seasoning to taste then press the mixture into the tomato shells. Wrap a small piece of cooking foil round the sides of each tomato then place them in a lightly greased ovenproof dish and bake in a moderately hot oven (190 C, 375 F, gas 5) for 40 minutes.

For the sauce, mix the soured cream with the chives and add nutmeg to taste. Transfer to a serving bowl, sprinkle the flaked almonds on top and chill until you are ready to serve the tomatoes. Garnish the tomatoes with watercress and serve, handing the sauce separately.
Serves 4

Note: beef tomatoes, also known as beefsteak tomatoes, are the very large tomatoes which are available from good greengrocers or some supermarkets. They weigh about 225 g/8 oz each, so each one when stuffed makes an adequate portion. Served on their own, these tomatoes are not remarkable for their flavour but their size makes them excellent for dishes such as this one.

Tahini is a paste made from sesame seeds, available from health-food shops, Greek shops and delicatessens.

Dolmades Fritters

This is an unusual way of preparing stuffed vine leaves, but it is very successful, the crisp outer covering concealing a superbly juicy filling. The quantities can be doubled if you like and the vine leaves can be served as a main dish, with salad and some cooked rice or pasta.

225 g/8 oz minced lamb
1 small onion, peeled and very
  finely chopped
1 teaspoon chopped tarragon
salt and freshly ground black
  pepper
50 g/2 oz Philadelphia cheese
12–14 vine leaves (from a
  packet or tin)

oil for deep frying
wedges of lemon to garnish
Batter
50 g/2 oz plain flour plus extra
  for coating
pinch of salt
1 large egg
100 ml/4 fl oz milk

Mix the lamb with the onion and tarragon, stir in seasoning to taste and add the cheese, mixing well to combine the ingredients evenly. Lay a vine leaf flat on a board. Take a small portion of the meat mixture (about the size of a walnut or slightly larger), then roll it into a ball and place it near the stalk end of the leaf. Fold the stalk end over the filling, then fold the sides in towards the middle. Roll the leaf from the folded end to make a neat package, enclosing the meat filling completely, and press the leaf firmly so that it stays in place. Continue filling the leaves in this way until all the mixture is used.

Now make the batter. Sift the flour into a bowl, add a pinch of salt and make a well in the middle. Add the egg, then gradually beat in the milk, working in the flour to make a smooth batter.

Heat the oil for deep frying to 180 C/350 F or until a cube of bread browns in 30 seconds. Dip each vine-leaf package first in flour, to coat it completely, then in the batter. Use a spoon and fork to cover the package completely in batter, taking care not to let them open at all; hold the ends firmly in place. Lift each one into the hot oil and cook until crisp and golden brown. Cook the vine leaves a few at a time then drain them on absorbent kitchen paper and keep hot until all are ready.

Serve the fritters on warmed individual plates with a couple of lemon wedges. The juice from the lemon is squeezed over the fritters just before they are eaten to balance the rich lamb and cream cheese filling – delicious! **Serves 4**

Spring Rolls

If you are preparing a very light main course, then offer two spring rolls per portion, but if your main course is substantial then one each will be ample. I suggest serving Sweet and Sour Mayonnaise (see page 171) with the rolls but you may well prefer to have them just as they are and savour the more authentic flavour.

2 Chinese dried mushrooms	*Dough*
225 g/8 oz minced pork	100 g/4 oz self-raising flour
a few drops of sesame oil	pinch of salt
1 (270-g/9½-oz) can bean	1 egg
sprouts, drained	2 tablespoons water
2 spring onions, chopped	*Garnish*
cayenne pepper	1 lettuce heart, shredded
2 tablespoons soy sauce	spring onion curls (page 31)
oil for deep frying	1 lemon, cut into wedges

Soak the mushrooms in hot water for 15 minutes. Meanwhile, place the pork and sesame oil in a frying pan and heat gently until it begins to cook, then dry fry the meat, stirring continuously, until lightly cooked. Drain the mushrooms and slice very thinly, then add them to the pork with the bean sprouts, spring onions and a sprinkling of cayenne pepper. Stir in the soy sauce and remove the pan from the heat. Leave the filling mixture to cool.

To make the dough, sift the flour into a bowl, add the salt and make a well in the middle. Beat the egg with the water then gradually mix it into the flour to make a stiff dough. Divide this into six equal portions and roll each into a 20-cm/8-in round. The rolled-out dough should be quite thin.

Put some of the filling in each circle, towards one end, brush the edge of the dough with a little water, then fold the end over the filling. Fold the sides over the filling, then roll up the dough from the filled end to make a neat roll. Make sure the end of the dough is well sealed.

Heat the oil for deep frying to 180 C/350 F or until a cube of bread browns in 30 seconds then deep fry the rolls, one or two at a time, until lightly browned. Drain on absorbent kitchen paper and keep hot until all are ready. Serve the rolls as soon as they are all cooked, arranging them on a serving dish with the shredded lettuce, onion curls and lemon wedges. **Makes 6**

Opposite page *Top: Herb Pâté (page 13); Below: Rich Pork Pâté (page 12)* **Overleaf** *Clockwise from top left: Stuffed Pitta Bread with Sesame Yogurt Sauce (page 18), Beef Canapés (page 16) and Veal and Roquefort Croquettes (page 17)*

Pork and Peanut Balls with Guacamole

(Illustrated opposite and on front cover)

Tiny pork meatballs flavoured with garlic and peanuts go very well with a chilled avocado dip. You can make the meatballs well in advance and keep them chilled to fry at the last minute but do not make the guacamole (dip) more than a couple of hours in advance, then sprinkle a little lemon juice over the surface, cover with cling film, and keep chilled until you are ready to serve it. Remember to give it a stir before serving it.

225 g/8 oz minced pork
1 small onion, peeled and very
   finely chopped or minced
50 g/2 oz unroasted peanuts,
   very finely chopped
25 g/1 oz fresh breadcrumbs
1 teaspoon ground cumin
½ teaspoon chilli powder
1 large clove garlic, peeled and
   crushed
2 tablespoons milk
salt and freshly ground black
   pepper

oil for deep frying
Guacamole
2 ripe avocado pears
juice of ½ small lemon
½ teaspoon chilli powder
2 tablespoons olive oil
2 tomatoes, peeled, seeded and
   finely chopped
½ cucumber to garnish

Put the pork in a basin and mix in all the remaining ingredients for the meatballs, adding plenty of seasoning. Make sure all the ingredients are thoroughly combined, then shape the mixture into 20 small meatballs and chill thoroughly.

For the guacamole, mash the avocados with the lemon juice and chilli powder, then beat in the olive oil and seasoning to taste. Stir in the tomatoes and chill lightly.

Heat the oil for deep frying to 180 C/350 F or until a cube of bread browns in 30 seconds. Fry the meatballs until they are lightly browned, then drain on absorbent kitchen paper and arrange on four individual plates. Halve lengthways and thinly slice the cucumber, then toss the slices together and put some round the meatballs on each plate. Serve at once, handing the guacamole separately. The meatballs can be dipped into the avocado mixture or it can be spooned on to the side of the plate with them. **Serves 4**

Top: Pork and Peanut Balls with Guacamole; Below: Philadelphia Meatballs (page 15)

Pork and Prawn Dim Sum

(Illustrated on page 68)

Dim sum are Chinese snacks, and the category can include all sorts of different dishes which are served in small quantities between meals. Typical are small dumplings and pastries which are usually steamed, for example these little pasties with a minced pork and prawn filling. They can be prepared well in advance and chilled until you are ready to cook them, but once cooked they should be served as soon as possible. The little dumplings are picked up and dipped in sauce before being eaten, or a little of the sauce can be dripped over them first.

100 g/4 oz minced pork
100 g/4 oz peeled cooked
   prawns, chopped
1 teaspoon soy sauce
1 tablespoon finely chopped
   spring onion
a few drops of sesame oil
Dough
100 g/4 oz plain flour
25 g/1 oz lard

50 ml/2 fl oz boiling water
Dipping sauce
4 tablespoons light soy sauce
1 small clove garlic, peeled and
   crushed
2 tablespoons lemon juice
Garnish
spring onion curls (see right)
cucumber slices, halved

First prepare the filling: mix the pork with the prawns then add the soy sauce and spring onion. Add just a few drops of sesame oil to flavour the mixture but be careful not to overpower it. Make sure the ingredients are thoroughly combined.

Now make the dough. Sift the flour into a bowl, put the lard in a small basin then stir in the boiling water until the fat melts. Make a well in the centre of the flour, pour in the fat and water and gradually work in the flour to make a smooth dough. Knead the dough lightly in the bowl then divide it into 12 portions. Roll each portion out on a surface lightly sprinkled with cornflour. You should aim to roll thin circles measuring about 10 cm/4 in. in diameter. Place a little of the filling in the middle of each circle then dampen the edges, fold them over to make a small Cornish pasty shape, pinch the dough together well to seal in the filling then flute the edge of the pastry between your thumb and forefinger to make a frilly edge. Place the dim sum on a greased plate. They are now ready for steaming.

Either use a saucepan of boiling water with the steamer on top or steam the dim sum in a bamboo steamer over a wok or on a steaming rack in a wok. Whichever method you use, cook them over rapidly boiling water for 15 minutes. When cooked the dough will be soft and glossy.

While the dim sum are cooking mix together the ingredients for the dipping sauce and put it in a small dish. Carefully arrange the cooked dim sum on individual plates and add a garnish of curled spring onions and cucumber slices. Serve immediately the dim sum are cooked, offering chopsticks and large table napkins as eating implements. If you think your guests may have difficulties in using chopsticks, then have small forks ready! **Serves 4**

Spring Onion Curls

Take a spring onion and trim off the roots together with any damaged leaves. Cut off any very long green strips, then cut the onion into fine strips from top to bottom, leaving them all attached at the white end. Place the onion in a bowl of iced water and leave for at least 30 minutes or until the onion ends have curled up. They can be made the day before they are required and stored overnight in the refrigerator.

Other Oriental Garnishes

If you like, you can add a splendid array of garnishing ingredients to the dim sum. This could be made up of carefully arranged piles of fine strips of carrot, large white radish and green pepper. If you have a little more time to spare, then par-boil a large carrot and a potato. Cut both into thin slices, then use an attractive cocktail cutter to stamp out flower or leaf shapes from the softened vegetables. These can be arranged on the platter with the dim sum and fine cucumber slices can be added to complete the garnish.

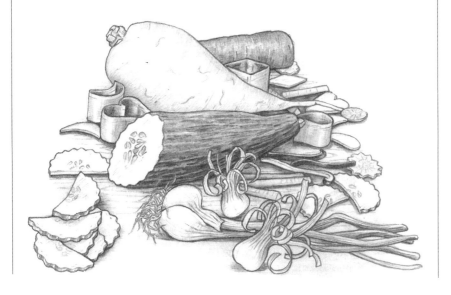

BURGERS, MEATBALLS AND SAUSAGES

The Basic Burger

More so than with any other mince recipe, the taste of a burger depends on the quality of the meat used to make it, but there is one other important factor in achieving good results, the cooking method – a charcoal grilled burger offering the best flavour.

Whether the meat used is beef, lamb or pork (and all three make excellent burgers) it should be lean, finely and evenly minced. If you have a good butcher and you know the quality of his meat is always reliable, then you are lucky – your burgers will almost certainly taste good. If you have any doubts about the quality of ready minced meat, then buy the required quantity of a particular cut and ask for it to be minced finely, or you can mince the meat yourself if you prefer. Chuck steak, lean pork shoulder and trimmed shoulder of lamb can all be minced to give excellent burgers. Minced veal can also be used to make rather special burgers.

The best burgers are made simply from meat, with seasoning added but nothing else. About 175 g/6 oz of meat per burger is the average amount, 100 g/4 oz makes a smallish burger and 225 g/8 oz gives a substantial one – good if you're particularly hungry. Season the meat and divide it into the required number of portions, dampen your hands to prevent the meat from sticking to them, then take a portion and knead it well together. It is important to knead the meat thoroughly as this will bind it together. Shape the burger neatly (dampen your hands again if necessary), then brush it with a little oil for cooking.

Cook the burgers under a hot grill, making sure that the first side is well browned before turning the burger over to cook the second side. Alternatively, the burgers can be cooked over a barbecue – the flavour will be superb – or in a very hot frying pan, lightly greased with oil. The meat should be cooked quickly so that it is not dried out.

Serving a burger can be the simplest thing in the world or quite elaborate – whichever you prefer. To keep it simple, all you need is a soft bun for each burger. Split the bun and toast the cut side until golden. Top one piece with a crisp lettuce leaf (iceberg is best), then lay the freshly cooked burger on top and add some of your favourite pickle or mustard. Put the lid on and serve immediately. You may prefer to have pickled gherkin, sliced tomato and onion, mustard pickle or a mixture of ketchup and mustard with the burger. There are lots of ideas to try here; some make the basic burger rather special.

Basic Burger Ideas

Cheese Burger. Top the cooked burger with a thick slice of cheese – Cheddar or mozzarella for example – then grill until the cheese has melted. Serve in a toasted bun with pickles. For beef and pork.

Creamy Blue Cheese Burger. For each burger mash about 50 g/2 oz blue cheese (Danish blue, Roquefort or Dolcelatte) with 50 g/2 oz cream cheese. Pile the mixture on top of the cooked burger in a toasted bun. Serve with a green salad (see page 172). Good for beef and lamb.

Creamy Horseradish Burger. For each burger beat 1 teaspoon horseradish sauce into 50 g/2 oz cream cheese. Put the cooked burger on the bun, top with the cream cheese mixture and add the other half of the bun. Serve at once. Good for beef and lamb.

Bacon Burger. Top each cooked burger with a couple of bacon rolls before putting the top on the bun. To make the bacon rolls, cut the rinds off bacon rashers, then roll them up and put them on metal skewers. Cook under a hot grill until crisp. Good for beef and lamb.

Sunny-side Burger. Top each burger with a fried egg before putting the top on the bun. Good for beef and pork.

Brunch Burger. Top the cooked burger with a couple of cooked bacon rashers and a fried egg. Top with the lid of the bun and serve a chipolata sausage and fried tomatoes with each burger. Best for beef.

Garlic Mushroom Burger (Illustrated on pages 46/47). Cook some whole button mushrooms in a little butter with a crushed clove of garlic added. Allow 50 g/2 oz mushrooms for each burger. Serve the burger with hot French bread instead of the bun. Top with the mushrooms and add plenty of chopped parsley. Good for beef, lamb or pork.

Burgers Peperonata (Illustrated on pages 46/47). Serve the cooked burgers on a bed of buttered noodles instead of in a bun. Top with fried chopped red and green peppers and onion. Allow one each of red and green peppers and one large onion (also chopped) for every four burgers. Cook the vegetables in a little olive oil or butter and add a crushed clove of garlic. Stir in plenty of seasoning and a little chopped parsley. Good for beef, lamb or pork.

Provençal Burgers. Serve the burgers on a bed of cooked noodles or rice instead of in a bun. Fry a large chopped onion in olive oil with a crushed clove of garlic added. When the onion is soft pour in 1 (397-g/14-oz) can chopped tomatoes and heat through. Add seasoning and chopped parsley before pouring the sauce over the burgers. Enough for four burgers. Good for beef, lamb and pork, also veal.

Note: try mixing the ideas above, for example you could serve a burger topped with garlic mushrooms and a wine sauce; one topped with grilled cheese, bacon and fried egg would also be a great success. If you want to experiment with the more elaborate burgers then try some of the following recipes.

Pizza Burgers

These are good supper snacks. Make a salad with them if you want more than just a bite to eat.

675 g/1½ lb minced beef
salt and freshly ground black
    pepper
1 clove garlic, peeled and
    crushed
dash of Worcestershire sauce
oil for cooking

4 thick slices of bread to serve
Topping
4 tomatoes, sliced
4 spring onions, chopped
4 slices mozzarella cheese
1 (50-g/2-oz) can anchovy fillets
4 black olives

Mix the beef with the seasoning, garlic and Worcestershire sauce. Knead the meat thoroughly so that it binds together, then divide it into four equal portions and shape each into a fairly large, thin burger. Brush the burgers with a little oil then cook them under a hot grill until well browned on both sides.

   While the burgers are cooking cut the crusts off the bread and cut the middle into circles just larger than the burgers. When the burgers are cooked toast the pieces of bread on one side under the grill then put the burgers on the untoasted side. Top with tomato slices, spring onion and cheese, add the anchovy fillets and put an olive on each. Grill until the cheese melts and serve at once. **Serves 4**

Lamb Burgers with Tarragon Egg Sauce

Serve these burgers with potatoes – new or baked – and Spinach and Bacon Salad (see page 173).

675 g/1½ lb minced lamb
1 clove garlic, peeled and
    crushed
salt and freshly ground black
    pepper
oil for cooking

1 quantity Béchamel Sauce (page
    162)
4 hard-boiled eggs, chopped
1 tablespoon chopped fresh
    tarragon

Mix the lamb with the garlic and plenty of seasoning, knead thoroughly and shape it into four burgers. Brush these with a little oil and cook them under a hot grill until well browned on both sides.

   Meanwhile, make the sauce according to the recipe instructions and stir in the hard-boiled eggs. Add the tarragon and mix well. Arrange the burgers on a serving dish then pour a little of the sauce over. Serve at once, handing the remaining sauce separately. **Serves 4**

Schnitzel Burgers

Minced veal makes excellent burgers and can be used as a substitute in many of the recipes in this chapter. However, this recipe has been specially created for minced veal. Serve the burgers with new potatoes and some fresh green vegetables.

675 g/1½ lb minced veal
salt and freshly ground black
    pepper
1 egg, beaten
50 g/2 oz dried white
    breadcrumbs

oil for cooking
To serve
4 hard-boiled eggs
2 tablespoons chopped parsley
1 lemon, thinly sliced

Mix the veal with seasoning to taste, then knead it thoroughly to bind it together, divide it into four equal burgers, shape them and coat them all over first in beaten egg, then in breadcrumbs. Heat a little oil in a large frying pan, add the burgers and cook over a moderate heat until they are golden underneath. Turn and cook the other side until golden. Do not fry them too quickly or the coating will brown too fast.

Press the hard-boiled eggs through a sieve. When the burgers are cooked, arrange them on a warmed serving platter, add a garnish of egg, parsley and lemon and serve immediately. **Serves 4**

Veal Burgers Veronique

Serve either new potatoes or buttered noodles and a green salad (see page 172) with these rather special burgers.

675 g/1½ lb minced veal
salt and freshly ground black
    pepper
2 tablespoons chopped parsley
1 small onion, peeled and very
    finely chopped or minced
dash of lemon juice

50 g/2 oz butter
1 quantity White Wine Sauce
    (page 164)
100 g/4 oz seedless white grapes
    or large grapes, halved and
    seeds removed

Mix the veal with the seasoning to taste, add the parsley, onion and lemon juice and knead very thoroughly. Divide the mixture into four equal portions and shape into burgers.

Melt the butter in a large frying pan and cook the burgers until golden underneath, then turn and cook the other side until golden. Remove the burgers from the pan, drain on absorbent kitchen paper and arrange on a warmed serving dish.

Make the sauce according to the recipe instructions, stir in the grapes and cook for just a minute to heat them through. Pour the sauce over the burgers and serve at once. **Serves 4**

Avocado Chilli Burgers

(Illustrated on page 48)

Serve these burgers with lots of cooked rice mixed with sweet corn, and offer a green salad (see page 172) with them.

350 g/12 oz minced pork
350 g/12 oz minced beef
1 onion, peeled and finely
   chopped
1–2 teaspoons chilli powder
1 tablespoon ground cumin
salt and freshly ground black
   pepper

1 egg, beaten
50 g/2 oz fresh breadcrumbs
oil for cooking
Topping
2 large ripe avocado pears
a little lemon juice
150 ml/$\frac{1}{4}$ pint soured cream
paprika

Mix the pork and beef together with all the other ingredients, adding chilli powder to taste and plenty of seasoning. Shape the meat mixture into four burgers and brush them with a little oil. Cook the burgers under a hot grill until well browned on both sides.

Meanwhile, prepare the topping: halve the avocados and remove their stones. Peel the flesh, cut it into slices and sprinkle with a little lemon juice to prevent it from discolouring.

Arrange the burgers on a warmed serving dish. Top with the avocado slices, then pour the cream over and sprinkle a little paprika on top. Serve immediately. **Serves 4**

Cidered Pork Burgers

These burgers are good with baked potatoes. Offer some lightly cooked buttered cabbage with them to make a wholesome family meal.

675 g/1$\frac{1}{2}$ lb minced pork
salt and freshly ground black
   pepper
$\frac{1}{2}$ teaspoon rubbed sage
grated rind of 1 orange
50 g/2 oz fresh breadcrumbs
1 egg, beaten
50 g/2 oz butter

1 small onion, peeled and
   chopped
2 tablespoons plain flour
1 chicken stock cube
300 ml/$\frac{1}{2}$ pint dry cider
100 g/4 oz button mushrooms,
   sliced

Mix the pork with the seasoning to taste and the sage, stir in the orange rind and the breadcrumbs, then add the egg and mix well, making sure all the ingredients are thoroughly bound together. Shape into four burgers.

Melt the butter in a large frying pan and cook the burgers over a moderate heat until well browned underneath, then turn them over and cook the second side. Remove them from the pan, drain on absorbent kitchen paper, place on a warmed serving dish and keep hot.

Add the onion to the fat remaining in the pan and cook until soft but not browned. Stir in the flour, crumble in the stock cube, then gradually pour in the cider. Bring to the boil, stirring all the time, then add the mushrooms and cook for a minute. Taste and adjust the seasoning, then pour the sauce over the burgers and serve immediately. **Serves 4**

Burgers Tropicana

Serve these burgers with an unusual vegetable dish — try buttered sweet potatoes, for example. Boil sweet potatoes in their skins until they are tender (about 20 to 30 minutes) then peel and cut them into cubes. Dot with butter and serve sprinkled with a little grated nutmeg.

675 g/1½ lb minced pork
1 small onion, peeled and finely
   chopped
25 g/1 oz desiccated coconut
salt and freshly ground black
   pepper

1 clove garlic, peeled and
   crushed
1 egg, beaten
4 canned pineapple rings,
   thoroughly drained
oil for cooking

Put the pork in a basin and mix in the onion, coconut, seasoning to taste, garlic and egg. When all the ingredients are thoroughly bound together divide the mixture into four equal portions.

Taking one pineapple ring and one portion of the meat mixture, shape the meat into a burger around the fruit, completely enclosing it. Shape the other burgers in the same way, brush them with a little oil and cook under a hot grill until well browned on both sides. Serve immediately. **Serves 4**

Pork and Peach Burgers
Instead of using pineapple rings in the above recipe, substitute drained, canned peach halves. Omit the coconut coating, then cook the burgers under a moderately hot grill, allowing plenty of time for the meat to cook through.

Devilled Pork Burgers

You can make beef or lamb burgers equally as well from this recipe. Serve chipped or sauté potatoes or cooked rice with the burgers. As an addition Avocado and Orange Salad (page 173) might go very well.

675 g/1½ lb minced pork
1 teaspoon chilli powder
1 tablespoon concentrated
   tomato purée
1 clove garlic, peeled and
   crushed
salt and freshly ground black
   pepper

dash of Worcestershire sauce
1 tablespoon made English
   mustard
oil for cooking
To serve
4 burger buns
150 ml/¼ pint strained Greek
   yogurt

Mix the pork with all the other ingredients (apart from the yogurt), divide into four equal portions and knead into burgers. Brush with a little oil and cook under a hot grill until well browned on both sides.

While the burgers are cooking split and toast the buns. Put a burger on each bun and top with a little yogurt before putting the top on. Serve immediately, offering the remaining yogurt separately. **Serves 4**

Walnut Burgers

Chopped walnuts and fresh herbs enliven simple pork burgers. Served with Rich Red Wine Sauce (page 164) these burgers would taste good with creamed potatoes and fresh vegetables or a salad. If you have the time, cream the potatoes, then pipe them in large swirls round the edge of the warmed serving dish so that the burgers can be arranged in the middle and the sauce poured over.

675 g/1½ lb minced pork
salt and freshly ground black
   pepper
100 g/4 oz walnuts, chopped
2 tablespoons chopped fresh
   herbs, for example, parsley,
   thyme, sage and rosemary

oil for cooking
Rich Red Wine Sauce (page 164)
   to serve

Mix the pork with the seasoning to taste. Add the nuts and herbs, then knead the meat thoroughly so that it is well bound together. Divide into four equal portions and shape into burgers. Brush with a little oil, and cook them a hot grill.

While the burgers are cooking make the sauce according to the recipe instructions. Serve the burgers immediately they are cooked, on a warmed platter with some of the sauce poured over them and the remainder handed separately. **Serves 4**

Prawn-dressed Pork Burgers

(Illustrated on page 48)

These burgers have a hint of the Orient about them. Seasoned with soy sauce and sesame oil, the pork is also flavoured with spring onions. With their splendid topping of prawns and chillies, they make a really special meal. Serve cooked Chinese egg noodles and a green salad with bean sprouts added to complete the theme.

675 g/1½ lb minced pork
2 tablespoons soy sauce
a few drops of sesame oil
bunch of spring onions,
   chopped
oil for cooking

Topping
1 green chilli
1 clove garlic, peeled and
   crushed
225 g/8 oz peeled cooked prawns

Mix the pork with the soy sauce, sesame oil and spring onions. Knead the mixture together well and divide it into four burgers. Brush these with a little oil and cook them under the grill until they are well browned on both sides.

Cut the stalk end off the chilli, then remove all the seeds from inside and cut the green part into very fine rings. Heat a little oil in a frying pan and cook the chilli rings and garlic for a few minutes, stirring continuously. Add the prawns and heat through.

Arrange the burgers on a warmed serving dish and spoon the prawns over the top. Serve at once. **Serves 4**

Note. You can, if you like, add more ingredients to the prawn topping. Fine strips of red or green peppers, sliced canned water chestnuts and pieces of canned pineapple can all be lightly stir-fried with the chilli and garlic before the prawns are added. If you are keen on spicy oriental food, add a couple of tablespoons of grated fresh root ginger and a pinch of five spice powder to the burger mixture.

Making Meatballs

Unlike the mixture for burgers, to make sure that the meatballs retain their shape as they cook, the ingredients usually consist of egg (or a small amount of other liquid) and breadcrumbs. The mixture should be kneaded thoroughly before it is shaped, then dampen your hands well before forming the meatballs so that the mixture does not stick to them. When you cook the meatballs, use two spoons to roll them gently in the pan so that they brown evenly. Once you pour liquid into the pan do not turn the meatballs unless the recipe suggests that you do. Cooked or raw, the meatballs will freeze well and they should be cooked from frozen if necessary. Well-seasoned meatballs in a good sauce can be served with rice or pasta to make a delicious meal. If you are at all worried that a bowl of meatballs will look slightly mundane, then add a colourful garnish of chopped fresh herbs, a sprinkling of chopped red pepper or a little paprika.

Meatball Fricassée

Serve this white meatball stew on a bed of freshly cooked green noodles and don't forget the paprika garnish.

450 g/1½ lb minced veal
salt and freshly ground black
   pepper
50 g/2 oz fresh breadcrumbs
2 small onions, peeled and
   chopped
100 g/4 oz button mushrooms,
   finely chopped
1 egg, beaten

50 g/2 oz butter
1 (390-g/13¾-oz) can artichoke
   hearts
225 g/8 oz small new potatoes,
   parboiled and drained
300 ml/½ pint dry white wine
1 chicken stock cube
150 ml/¼ pint single cream

Mix the veal with seasoning to taste, then add the breadcrumbs, half the onion, the chopped mushrooms and the egg. Mix together thoroughly then shape the mixture into 16 meatballs.

Melt the butter in a large flameproof casserole or heavy-based saucepan. Add the remaining onion and the meatballs and fry, turning occasionally, until the meatballs are lightly browned. Stir in the artichoke hearts and the potatoes and cook for one minute. Pour in the wine and crumble in the stock cube, then bring gently to the boil. Just as the liquid boils reduce the heat so that it is just simmering and cover the pan. Cook gently for 30 minutes.

Taste the sauce and add seasoning, then stir in the cream and heat gently without allowing the sauce to boil. Serve immediately. **Serves 4**

Neapolitan Meatballs

Dishes from the southern region of Italy tend to be rich in the use of olive oil, garlic and tomatoes and are most frequently served with pasta, particularly spaghetti. Here, simple meatballs are cooked in an equally plain but full-flavoured sauce which echoes the flavour of the Neapolitan region.

225 g/8 oz minced beef
225 g/8 oz minced pork
salt and freshly ground black
   pepper
50 g/2 oz fresh breadcrumbs
1 egg, beaten
4 tablespoons chopped parsley
4 tablespoons olive oil
Sauce
1 large onion, peeled and
   chopped
2 cloves garlic, peeled and
   crushed
1 medium carrot, chopped

2 sticks celery, chopped
bay leaf
2 tablespoons plain flour
1 (397-g/14-oz) can chopped
   tomatoes
1 beef stock cube
2 tablespoons concentrated
   tomato purée
600 ml/1 pint red wine
To serve
350 g/12 oz spaghetti
freshly grated Parmesan cheese
2 tablespoons chopped parsley

Mix the beef and pork in a bowl. Add plenty of seasoning then mix in the breadcrumbs and egg until all the ingredients are thoroughly combined. Finally stir in the parsley. Shape the mixture into 16 meatballs.

Heat the olive oil in a large frying pan which has a lid or in a saucepan. Add the meatballs and fry them, turning them over once or twice, until browned all over. Remove them from the pan and set them aside on absorbent kitchen paper.

Add the onion, garlic, carrot and celery to the pan and fry until the onion is soft but not browned. Stir in the bay leaf and flour, then pour in the tomatoes and crumble in the stock cube. Stir in the tomato purée and pour in the wine, still stirring. Bring to the boil, then replace the meatballs in the sauce and cover the pan. Simmer gently for 30 minutes.

While the meatballs are cooking, cook the spaghetti in plenty of boiling salted water. Drain the spaghetti and turn it into a large serving dish. Pour the meatballs over and sprinkle with a little Parmesan cheese and the parsley. Serve immediately. **Serves 4**

Meatball Goulash

Meatballs are often sadly underestimated and looked upon as being little better than poor-quality sausages. This is most unjust, as homemade meatballs can be extremely interesting, even a simple recipe such as this one tasting good and satisfying. Serve plenty of buttered noodles with the meatballs.

450 g/1 lb minced beef
50 g/2 oz fresh breadcrumbs
1 egg
1 teaspoon thyme
salt and freshly ground black
  pepper
2 tablespoons oil
1 large red or green pepper

1 large onion, peeled and sliced
1 tablespoon plain flour
1 tablespoon paprika
beef stock cube
300 ml/$\frac{1}{2}$ pint tomato juice
300 ml/$\frac{1}{2}$ pint red wine
150 ml/$\frac{1}{4}$ pint natural yogurt
2 tablespoons chopped parsley

Mix the beef with the breadcrumbs, egg and thyme, adding seasoning to taste. Shape the mixture into 12 equal meatballs. If you dampen your hands and keep them damp as you shape the mixture you will find that it does not stick.

Heat the oil in a large frying pan or heavy-based saucepan and add the meatballs, frying them until they are browned all over. Cut the stalk end off the pepper, remove all the seeds and pith from inside then cut into thin slices. Remove the meatballs from the pan and fry the onion and pepper gently in the remaining fat until the onion is soft but not browned. Stir in the flour and paprika, crumble in the stock cube and add the tomato juice. Pour in the wine, still stirring, and bring to the boil. Replace the meatballs in the pan and simmer gently, covered, for 30 minutes.

To serve, transfer the meatballs with their sauce to a heated serving dish, swirl the yogurt into the sauce and sprinkle the parsley on top. Serve at once. **Serves 4**

Note. Meatball Goulash also tastes excellent if the meatballs are made of minced pork or veal, or a mixture of both. Chopped rindless streaky bacon, fried with the meatballs, and sliced button mushrooms, added towards the end of the cooking time, are both flavoursome ingredients which can be added to vary the dish.

Meatballs-in-the-hole

This is a variation on that old favourite, toad-in-the-hole. Serve Onion Gravy (below) with the cooked dish and offer some simple vegetable accompaniments – cooked cabbage, creamed or baked potatoes or carrots.

450 g/1 lb minced beef
50 g/2 oz fresh breadcrumbs
generous dash of Worcestershire
   sauce
1 teaspoon dried mixed herbs
1 egg
2 tablespoons chopped parsley

salt and freshly ground black
   pepper
Batter
100 g/4 oz plain flour
2 eggs
300 ml/$\frac{1}{2}$ pint milk

Put the mince in a bowl, then add the breadcrumbs, Worcestershire sauce, herbs, egg, parsley and seasoning to taste. Mix thoroughly until all the ingredients are well combined then shape the mixture into eight meatballs. Place these in a greased ovenproof dish.

For the batter, sift the flour into a bowl, add a pinch of salt and make a well in the middle. Break the eggs into the well and gradually beat in the flour, at the same time pouring in the milk little by little. Beat thoroughly to make a smooth, light batter, then pour it round, not over, the meatballs. Bake in a moderately hot oven (190 C, 375 F, gas 5) for 55 to 60 minutes. When cooked, the batter should be risen and golden brown. Serve at once. **Serves 4**

Onion Gravy

To make an onion gravy, fry a large onion (sliced into thin rings) in a little beef dripping, butter, lard or oil until lightly browned. Do this slowly so that the onion does not burn. Stir in 3 tablespoons plain flour, then crumble in 1 beef stock cube and gradually pour in 350 ml/$\frac{3}{4}$ pint boiling water. Bring to the boil, then simmer gently for 20 minutes. Stir in a little gravy browning before serving.

Meatballs Bourguignonne

(Illustrated opposite)

Serve these meatballs in rich wine sauce with plenty of buttered noodles and a green salad (see page 172).

450 g/1 lb minced beef
100 g/4 oz lean rindless bacon, chopped
2 tablespoons chopped parsley
pinch of thyme
generous pinch of ground mace
1 egg, beaten
50 g/2 oz fresh breadcrumbs
salt and freshly ground black pepper
50 g/2 oz butter

450 g/1 lb pickling onions, peeled and left whole
1 large clove garlic, peeled and crushed
225 g/8 oz button mushrooms
2 tablespoons plain flour
300 ml/$\frac{1}{2}$ pint full-bodied red wine
1 beef stock cube
2 tablespoons concentrated tomato purée

Mix the meat with the bacon, herbs, mace, egg and breadcrumbs. Add plenty of seasoning to the mixture. Knead the ingredients together so that they are well mixed, then shape the mixture into 16 meatballs.

Melt the butter in a flameproof casserole or heavy-based saucepan. Add the pickling onions, garlic and meatballs and cook, turning the meatballs occasionally, until they are browned all over. By this time the onions should also be softened. Add the mushrooms to the pan and stir well over a moderate heat for a few minutes. Sprinkle the flour into the pan and stir in the wine. Crumble in the stock cube and add the tomato purée. Bring to the boil, stirring all the time. Reduce the heat as soon as the sauce boils, then put a lid on the pan and simmer gently for 30 minutes. Serve piping hot. **Serves 4**

Opposite page *Top: Greek-style Kebabs (page 49); Below: Meatballs Bourguignonne* **Overleaf** *Clockwise from top right: Burgers Peperonata, Garlic Mushroom Burgers, a cheese burger with bacon rolls and a basic burger (all on pages 32/33)*

Greek-style Kebabs

(Illustrated on page 45)

Serve these full-flavoured, juicy kebabs with a Greek salad (see page 174) and some warmed pitta bread. Baked potatoes or pasta would also go very well. Double the quantities if you are expecting the diners to be especially hungry.

450 g/1 lb minced lamb
1 onion, peeled and finely
   chopped
1 tablespoon ground coriander
1 large clove garlic, peeled and
   crushed
1 teaspoon marjoram
½ teaspoon thyme
50 g/2 oz fresh breadcrumbs

1 tablespoon lemon juice
salt and freshly ground black
   pepper
Garnish
1 lettuce heart
1 lemon, cut into wedges
1 small onion, peeled and thinly
   sliced

Place the lamb in a bowl, then add the onion, coriander and garlic. Mix thoroughly and add all the remaining ingredients, including seasoning (the mixture should be well seasoned). Stir thoroughly so that the spices and herbs are evenly distributed, then form into 16 meatballs. Thread them on to four skewers, flattening them slightly so that they are elongated and then chill thoroughly.

Just before you are ready to eat, cook the kebabs under a very hot grill for about 15 minutes, turning them once or twice. Wash the lettuce and arrange the leaves on individual plates, then lay the kebabs on top. Add the lemon wedges to garnish and separate the onion slices into rings before sprinkling them over the top. Serve at once. **Serves 4**

Top: Prawn-dressed Pork Burgers (page 39); Below: Avocado Chilli Burgers (page 36)

Creamed Somerset Meatballs

This is a good economical way of making a special dinner party dish. Admittedly the cream is not a cheap item but using cider instead of wine helps with the cost and the result is as good as any dish made with a more expensive cut of meat. The secret is in the presentation of the food, so offer an imaginative salad with the meatballs – try combining the Avocado and Orange Salad with a green salad (see pages 173 and 172).

450 g/1 lb minced pork
salt and freshly ground black
  pepper
50 g/2 oz fresh breadcrumbs
1 egg, beaten
$\frac{1}{2}$ teaspoon rubbed sage
4 tablespoons chopped parsley
2 tablespoons oil

1 large onion, peeled and
  chopped
225 g/8 oz button mushrooms
2 tablespoons plain flour
300 ml/$\frac{1}{2}$ pint dry cider
1 chicken stock cube
150 ml/$\frac{1}{4}$ pint single cream

Mix the pork with seasoning to taste, then add the breadcrumbs, egg, sage and half the parsley. Mix thoroughly then shape into 12 meatballs.

Heat the oil in a flameproof casserole or heavy-based saucepan. Add the onion and the meatballs and cook until the meatballs are lightly browned and the onion is soft. Stir in the mushrooms and cook for a minute, then add the flour and stir in the cider. Crumble in the stock cube and bring to the boil, then reduce the heat and cover the pan. Simmer gently for 30 minutes.

Taste the sauce and add more seasoning if necessary, then stir in the cream and heat gently for a couple of minutes. Sprinkle the remaining parsley over the meatballs and serve at once. **Serves 4**

Creamy Meatball Gratin

The Creamy Somerset Meatballs can be presented most attractively if they are spooned into a ring of piped mashed potato. Pipe the potatoes round the edge of an ovenproof gratin dish, then put the meatballs in the middle. Top with a mixture of grated cheese and breadcrumbs, half and half, then cook under a hot grill until golden. Sprinkle a little chopped parsley over the gratin before it is served.

Crepinette

These, the French equivalent of faggots, are usually made with all sorts of different offal minced up with some meat, but this recipe has been adapted to the slightly more conservative tastes of the British cook. Minced pork is taken as the basic ingredient, then some finely chopped kidney and liver are added with a selection of herbs and seasonings. The result is very tasty, particularly when served with Onion Gravy (see page 43) or Tomato Sauce (see page 163).

100 g/4 oz lambs' kidneys
225 g/8 oz lamb's liver
450 g/1 lb minced pork
2 onions, peeled and finely
   chopped
1 or 2 cloves garlic, peeled and
   crushed
2 teaspoons dried thyme
2 sprigs fresh rosemary

2 sprigs fresh sage
1 bay leaf
4 tablespoons chopped fresh
   parsley
salt and freshly ground black
   pepper
1 egg
100 g/4 oz fresh breadcrumbs
50 g/2 oz butter

Cut the kidneys in half horizontally, then use a pair of kitchen scissors to snip out the white cores. Finely chop the liver and prepared kidneys, then add them to the pork in a fairly large bowl. Stir in the onion and garlic and add the thyme. Chop the fresh herbs (including the bay leaf) and add them to the meat with the parsley and plenty of seasoning. Mix in the egg and make sure all the ingredients are well combined. Take spoonfuls of the mixture (it should be fairly soft), roll it into balls and coat them completely in the breadcrumbs.

   Put the crepinettes on a large greased baking tray or roasting tin and dot each one with butter. Bake in a moderately hot oven (200 C, 400 F, gas 6) for 50 to 60 minutes. The cooked breadcrumb coating should be crisp and golden. Serve at once. **Serves 4**

Homemade Sausages

Homemade sausages are certainly not too difficult to make and they are so far superior to most bought sausages that they are well worth the effort involved. You may find the thought of obtaining and filling sausage skins too daunting a prospect for you – but don't give up.

The first step is to find a good butcher who makes his own sausages, as he may be willing to sell you some sausage skins. He may only be able to offer you a large carton (about 100 yards in length!) in which case you will have to decide whether you are going to make vast quantities of sausages and freeze them or, more sensibly, encourage a friend to go halves with you and split the carton. Natural sausage skins are salted and they will keep in an airtight container in the bottom of the refrigerator for two to three months. Alternatively, forget about making sausages in skins and try some of the other suggestions which I give below.

Filling sausage skins. If you have a special sausage filler attachment for your food mixer (available only with the large models), then you have no problems, just follow the manufacturer's instructions. Otherwise, take lengths of the sausage skin – don't be over ambitious but cut off about 91 cm/3 ft – and soak them in cold water for at least 30 minutes, overnight if you wish. The skins will expand, soften and become paler in colour. Drain off the water, add fresh and wash the skins by swirling them gently with your fingers. Repeat this process to remove all the salt, then pour in enough fresh water to keep the skins covered.

You will need a large piping bag and a large plain nozzle about 1–2.5 cm/$\frac{1}{2}$–1 in. in diameter. Fit the nozzle in the bag, then put some of the sausage mixture into the bag, pressing it well down to the end of the nozzle. If you have an empty nozzle at the end of the bag, the skin will fill with air as you squeeze out the mixture and blow up like a small balloon. Do not overfill the bag or it may be too difficult for you to squeeze.

Take a length of sausage skin, find the end, and open it carefully. With the filled bag resting on the work surface, gradually push the sausage skin on to the nozzle, using your right hand to guide the skin as far up the nozzle (and the outside of the piping bag) as possible, and pushing more on with your left hand. When most of the skin is on the nozzle you can start to carefully squeeze out the mixture, but only a little at first. When you have a small portion of mixture in the skin, then tie a small neat knot in the end.

The trick in filling sausages is to squeeze out the mixture and allow enough of the skin to run off the end of the nozzle at the same time so as to produce sausages which are nice and full but not ready to burst. Squeeze the bag with your right hand, at the same time using your left hand to guide the sausage skin evenly off the nozzle. The main thing to remember is that it sounds far more difficult than it really is! Once you've filled one length of skin you will have got the knack. When you have a length of sausage you can either twist it at intervals to make individual sausages or curl it round into one large sausage (like a Cumberland sausage).

Keeping sausages. The sausages can be kept in the refrigerator for a few days or they can be frozen for up to 6 months. A word of warning, however. I was very excited about the first batch of sausages I ever made. Highly seasoned, with lashings of garlic, they tasted delicious, so I froze lots of them and even though they were double packed the freezer reeked of garlic the whole time they were in there!

Cooking sausages. Sausages packed in natural skins should not be pricked before they are cooked. They should be cooked fairly slowly so that the filling has time to cook through, then until the skin is crisp and evenly golden. A frying pan over a moderate heat or under a moderate grill are both fine, but the sausages will be at their best baked slowly in the oven. Drain the cooked sausages quickly on absorbent kitchen paper, then serve them at once or allow them to cool completely.

Skinless sausages. If you would prefer to avoid sausage skins altogether, simply shape the mixture into sausage shapes and coat them in flour. They can then be cooked as they are. A coating of egg and breadcrumbs can be added and the sausages can be fried or coated in a light batter and deep fried.

The Basic Pork Sausage

This is a plain, lightly seasoned pork mixture to which you can add any other ingredients you fancy for the sausages. For instance, try emphasising the herbs by adding more of one in particular or mixed fresh herbs. Additional spices, garlic, wine or beer can be mixed in or finely chopped gammon can be included to give the result a meaty bite. Use your imagination and you could well create your own unique family sausage recipe.

450 g/1 lb minced pork
75 g/3 oz fresh breadcrumbs
1 teaspoon dried mixed herbs
$\frac{1}{2}$ teaspoon ground mace
a little freshly grated nutmeg

$\frac{1}{2}$ teaspoon ground coriander
salt and freshly ground black
 pepper
about 100 ml/4 fl oz water

Mix the pork with all the other ingredients, being generous with the seasoning and stirring in the water to make the mixture soft enough to pipe without too much difficulty. Fill the sausage skins according to the instructions given above. **Serves 4**

Pork and Beef Sausages

These are simple, meaty sausages which would do a toad-in-the-hole more than its fair share of justice!

225 g/8 oz minced pork
225 g/8 oz minced beef
½ teaspoon thyme
½ teaspoon marjoram
1 teaspoon chopped chives
½ teaspoon ground mace
½ teaspoon rubbed sage

salt and freshly ground black
   pepper
1 teaspoon mustard powder
75 g/2 oz fresh breadcrumbs
1 beef stock cube
100 ml/4 fl oz boiling water

Place the minced meats in a bowl, then add all the remaining ingredients except the stock cube and water. Dissolve the cube in the water, then stir the liquid into the sausage mixture. Make sure that all the ingredients are thoroughly and evenly combined, then fill the sausage skins according to the instructions given on page 52. **Serves 4**

Beef and Tomato Sausages

The idea for beef and tomato sausages is certainly not an original one, indeed I believe they are a traditional speciality from the north of England. Anyway this is no ancient family recipe, just a mixture I made up myself; if you would prefer plain beef sausages, then omit the tomato purée.

450 g/1 lb minced beef
1 small onion, peeled and very
   finely chopped or minced
4 teaspoons ground coriander
1 teaspoon dried thyme
4 tablespoons concentrated
   tomato purée
1 tablespoon Worcestershire
   sauce

generous sprinkling of freshly
   grated nutmeg
75 g/3 oz fresh breadcrumbs
salt and freshly ground black
   pepper
1 beef stock cube
150 ml/¼ pint boiling water

Mix all the ingredients except the stock cube and water in a bowl. Dissolve the stock cube in the water then stir it into the meat mixture. Make sure that all the ingredients are thoroughly and evenly combined, then fill the sausage skins according to the instructions given on page 52. **Serves 4**

Garlic Pork Sausages

This recipe makes sausages with a good garlic flavour, ideal for barbecues. The sausages can also be cooked and cooled, then served cut into thin slices. If you would like to make the sausages with just a hint of garlic, then reduce the quantities accordingly.

450 g/1 lb minced pork
75 g/3 oz fresh breadcrumbs
4 cloves garlic, peeled and
  crushed
2 teaspoons marjoram
1 teaspoon thyme
1 teaspoon paprika
1 teaspoon ground mace

1 very small onion, peeled and
  minced or grated
salt and freshly ground black
  pepper
150 ml/$\frac{1}{4}$ pint full-bodied red
  wine (or try red vermouth,
  it's excellent)

Place the pork in a bowl and break it up slightly, then add all the other ingredients and mix thoroughly until they are well combined. Put the mixture into a piping bag fitted with a large plain nozzle and fill the sausage skins according to the instructions on page 52. **Serves 4**

Continental-style Sausages

This is my 'way-over-the-top' sausage recipe – if you like full-flavoured foods, then this is the one to try.

225 g/8 oz minced pork
225 g/8 oz minced beef
100 g/4 oz rindless streaky
  bacon, chopped
1 small onion, peeled and
  chopped
50 g/2 oz fresh breadcrumbs
1 tablespoon capers, chopped
1 tablespoon green peppercorns,
  lightly crushed

2 cloves garlic, peeled and
  crushed
2 teaspoons ground coriander
$\frac{1}{2}$ teaspoon ground cinnamon
1 teaspoon thyme
1 teaspoon marjoram
1 teaspoon rubbed sage
salt and freshly ground black
  pepper
6 tablespoons cream sherry

Put the meats and bacon in a bowl, then gradually mix in all the remaining ingredients and stir until thoroughly combined, making sure that all the spices and herbs are evenly distributed. Put the mixture into a piping bag fitted with a large plain nozzle and fill the sausage skins according to the instructions on page 52. **Serves 4**

HOT FROM THE POT

One of the great advantages of mince is that it can be cooked comparatively quickly and easily on top of the cooker, without heating up the oven or standing over a flaming hot grill. For those times when you want to conjure up a one-pot meal or if your cooking facilities are limited to the minimum, then take note of some of the recipe ideas in this chapter – you may find them interesting.

Simple Mince Supper

There is nothing wrong with serving a very simple pot of cooked mince providing that you make some sort of imaginative addition, like the slices of bread in this recipe. Listed below are some more ideas for tarting up the most simple of mince pots.

2 tablespoons oil
1 clove garlic, peeled and
   crushed
1 large onion, peeled and
   chopped
450 g/1 lb minced beef
salt and freshly ground black
   pepper
2 tablespoons plain flour
1 beef stock cube

600 ml/1 pint water, beer or red
   wine
225 g/8 oz carrots, sliced
100 g/4 oz mushrooms, sliced
Topping
100 g/4 oz Cheddar cheese,
   grated
2 tablespoons French mustard
½ French loaf, sliced

Heat the oil in a flameproof casserole. Add the garlic and onion and cook until the onion is soft but not browned. Stir in the mince and continue to cook, stirring all the time, until the meat is browned. Add seasoning and stir in the plain flour. Crumble in the stock cube and pour in the water, beer or wine. Bring to the boil, then add the carrots. Cover and simmer over a moderate heat for 20 minutes. Add the mushrooms, taste and adjust the seasoning, then simmer for a further 10 minutes.

   Meanwhile, beat the cheese with the mustard until thoroughly combined and softened, and spread over the bread slices. When the mince is ready, overlap the bread on top and put it under a hot grill until golden and bubbling. Serve at once. **Serves 4**

More Basic Mince Ideas

Spicy Mince with Eggs. Cook some minced beef or pork with chopped onion, adding mushrooms and a little stock. Stir in about a tablespoon paprika to each 450 g/1 lb mince and add a can of tomatoes. Serve the cooked mince on boiled rice and top each portion with a fried egg.

Mince with Chick Peas. Cook minced lamb or pork as in the main recipe but omit the carrots. Stir in a can or two of chick peas with the mushrooms. Swirl some natural yogurt into the cooked mince just before it is served.

Mince-stuffed Potatoes. Cook a basic mince mixture using about half the required liquid. You can use beef or pork. Serve the mince in cut baked potatoes and top each portion with lots of grated cheese and some chopped parsley.

Gratin of Mince. Make a full-flavoured mince mixture then turn it into a serving dish and pour Cheese Sauce (see page 162) on top. Sprinkle breadcrumbs and more grated cheese over the sauce then grill the top.

Barbecued Mince with Beans

Unlike the superior bean pots overleaf, this is really basic food – the sort of dish that the kids'll love! Once in a while it can also go down quite well with adults if served with piping hot baked potatoes.

1 large onion, peeled and chopped	2 tablespoons French mustard
1 clove garlic, peeled and crushed	1 (425-g/15-oz) can baked beans
2 tablespoons oil	1 (425-g/15-oz) can red kidney beans
450 g/1 lb minced beef	generous dash of Worcestershire sauce
salt and freshly ground black pepper	1 tablespoon dark brown sugar
1 (397-g/14-oz) can chopped tomatoes	

Fry the onion and garlic in the oil until the onion is soft but not browned. Add the mince and cook over a moderate heat, stirring continuously, until the meat is evenly browned. Add plenty of seasoning, then pour in the tomatoes and stir in the mustard. Add both cans of beans (the kidney beans make the dish more interesting, but add two cans of baked beans if you prefer!) and be generous with the Worcestershire sauce. Finally stir in the sugar.

Heat the mixture gently until it reaches simmering point, then put a lid on the pan and continue to cook very gently for about 30 minutes. Remove the lid, stir the mixture well and taste it to make sure it is seasoned adequately. Serve at once, with baked potatoes or plenty of bread. This mixture is also good on thick slices of hot buttered toast.
Serves 4

Three Bean Pots

For when I've got lots of other things to do I like to have a few ideas tucked up my sleeve for meals which I can throw together without fiddling around in the kitchen for hours on end. High on that list comes bean pots – one-pot dishes with meat, vegetables and filling ingredients all mixed up together in a wonderful stew. Ladled into sensible-sized bowls, these dishes always taste fantastic with lots of crusty bread and a salad. They can either be whizzed up in a flash if you're good at chopping and keep a supply of canned beans in the cupboard, or they can be prepared ages in advance for cooking away unattended if you use dried beans.

Take these three recipes as a guide and experiment with different types of beans (canned or dried), mixing them together if you like and adding plenty of seasonal vegetables if you want to make family-sized stews. The cooked dishes freeze well for a couple of months, so why not make large batches and freeze some for times when you can't think beyond defrosting and reheating an existing dish?

Chilli con Carne

I've tasted chilli con carne that I could eat for ever and I've tasted the most boring but hot concoctions that blow the roof off your mouth without leaving any hint of good food behind. In other words this is a dish which can be deliciously more-ish or unpleasantly tasteless! I hope you like this recipe as much as I do. Vary the quantities of chilli powder according to your own taste, but however much you add I think you will find that you will still be able to taste the other ingredients. Offer hot, crusty French bread (and plenty of it) with the chilli. You can, of course, use canned beans instead of dried if you don't want the bother of soaking beans overnight.

225 g/8 oz red kidney beans
salt and freshly ground black
   pepper
1 Spanish onion or 2 medium
   onions, peeled and chopped
225 g/8 oz rindless smoked
   streaky bacon, chopped
2 large cloves garlic, peeled and
   crushed
2 tablespoons ground coriander

1 tablespoon ground cumin
1 tablespoon chilli powder
450 g/1 lb minced beef
1 beef stock cube
600 ml/1 pint water
2 tablespoons concentrated
   tomato purée
2 tablespoons chopped fresh
   coriander leaves or parsley

Soak the beans overnight in sufficient cold water to cover them. Next day, drain the water off and put the beans in a large saucepan. Add plenty of water and a pinch of salt, then bring to the boil. Boil the beans for 2 minutes, then reduce the heat and cover the pan. Leave the beans to simmer gently for 30 minutes.

Put the onion and bacon in a large saucepan or flameproof casserole and heat gently until the fat runs from the bacon, then fry, stirring frequently, until the onion is soft but not browned. Add the garlic, coriander, cumin and chilli powder and cook for about a minute. Stir in the beef, breaking it up as it cooks. Cook until the meat is lightly browned all over, then crumble the stock cube into the pan and pour in the water. Stir in the tomato purée and seasoning to taste, then bring to the boil.

Drain the beans and add them to the pan, then bring back to the boil. Cover the pan, reduce the heat and simmer gently for about an hour, or until the beans are tender and much of the liquid has been absorbed. The cooked chilli should be juicy but not too runny. Stir in the coriander or parsley (coriander gives the best flavour so use it if you can find any) and serve at once. **Serves 4**

Pork and Beans

This is a good old favourite made with haricot beans – I have used dried beans soaked overnight, but you can substitute canned beans if you like and cut down the cooking time to about 15 minutes. If you do opt for canned beans, then remember to reduce the liquid – you will need about 300 ml/$\frac{1}{2}$ pint instead of the quantity below.

225 g/8 oz dried haricot beans
25 g/1 oz butter
1 large onion, peeled and
  chopped
450 g/1 lb minced pork
bay leaf

2 large sprigs of fresh sage
salt and freshly ground black
  pepper
1 chicken stock cube
900 ml/1$\frac{1}{2}$ pints water
plenty of chopped parsley

Soak the beans in plenty of cold water overnight. Next day drain them thoroughly and pick out any bad ones.

Melt the butter in a heavy-based saucepan and fry the onion until it is soft but not brown. Add the pork and fry it until lightly browned, stirring frequently to break up the meat and make sure it cooks evenly. Add the bay leaf and sage with plenty of seasoning. Crumble the stock cube and sprinkle it in then pour in the water and add the beans. Stir well, bring to the boil and reduce the heat so that the liquid is just simmering. Cover the pan and leave the bean pot to cook for 40 to 45 minutes.

Remove the lid from the pan and boil off any excess water – the bean pot should be quite moist but not too runny when it is served. Sprinkle in plenty of parsley and ladle the mixture into bowls. **Serves 4**

Note. You can add sliced carrots or cubed celeriac, shredded carrot or spinach to this bean pot. Add the root vegetables with the beans but leave the leaf vegetables until near the end of the cooking time.

Lamb with Flageolet Beans

(Illustrated on page 65)

Pale green flageolet beans are available in cans as well as dried, so again you can do a substitution trick if you do not want to be bothered with soaking beans overnight. This is one of my favourite bean and meat combinations because it's just a little bit unusual. Serve a salad of shredded chicory and celery, sprinkled with sesame seeds and a simple vinaigrette to go with the bean pot.

350 g/12 oz flageolet beans	1 tablespoon tarragon
1 tablespoon oil	salt and freshly ground black
1 large onion, peeled and	pepper
chopped	900 ml/1½ pints water
1 large clove garlic, peeled and	1 chicken stock cube
crushed	225 g/8 oz mushrooms, sliced
450 g/1 lb minced lamb	2 tablespoons chopped parsley
bay leaf	

Soak the beans overnight in plenty of cold water. Next day, drain them and pick out any bad ones.

Heat the oil in a large heavy-based saucepan or flameproof casserole. Add the onion and garlic and cook until the onion is soft but not browned. Add the lamb and fry it, stirring all the time, until lightly browned. Stir in the bay leaf, tarragon and plenty of seasoning. Pour in the water and crumble in the stock cube, then add the beans to the pan and bring to the boil.

Once the liquid is boiling, reduce the heat and cover the pan tightly, then simmer gently for about 50 to 60 minutes. If it is simmering quite gently there should be enough liquid to complete the cooking but it's a good idea to check about two-thirds of the way through. Stir the mushrooms into the bean pot about 5 minutes before the end of the cooking time. At the end of the time you should have virtually no cooking liquid left, but the mixture should be moist. Quickly stir in the parsley and offer a bowl of soured cream with the bean pot. **Serves 4**

Shepherd's Hot Pot

1 large onion, peeled and
  chopped
350 g/12 oz carrots, sliced
4 sticks of celery, sliced
2 tablespoons oil
450 g/1 lb minced lamb

1 lamb or beef stock cube
salt and freshly ground black
  pepper
600 ml/1 pint water
50 g/2 oz pearl barley

Fry the onion, carrots and celery in the oil until the onion is soft but not browned. Stir in the lamb and continue to cook until the meat is lightly browned. Stir the meat during cooking to break it up and make sure it is evenly cooked.

Crumble in the stock cube and add seasoning then pour in the water and add the pearl barley. Bring to the boil, reduce the heat so that the liquid simmers gently and cover the pan tightly. Simmer very gently for $1\frac{1}{4}$ hours. Check during cooking to make sure that there is still plenty of liquid in the pan – there should be ample if the hot pot is just simmering. When cooked it should resemble a thick soup. **Serves 4**

Note: you can add all sorts of vegetables to this hot pot. Try cubes of swede and parsnip, leeks or cabbage. If you do add a large variety of vegetables, then increase the quantity of meat by half as much again.

Savoury Omelette

This is the next step up from a Spanish omelette – a meaty meal in itself, it would also go very well with a dish of macaroni cheese.

25 g/1 oz butter
1 large onion, peeled and
  chopped
225 g/8 oz frozen mixed
  vegetables
450 g/1 lb minced beef
2 teaspoons dried mixed herbs

100 g/4 oz Cheddar cheese,
  grated
4 eggs, beaten
4 tablespoons milk
salt and freshly ground black
  pepper

Melt the butter in a large non-stick frying pan, then add the onion and cook until it is very soft but not browned. Stir in the vegetables and meat all at once and continue to cook until the meat is lightly browned. Stir in the mixed herbs and cheese. Quickly beat the eggs with the milk and plenty of seasoning, then pour the mixture into the pan. Stir thoroughly and cook fairly gently until the eggs are almost set and browned underneath.

Heat the grill and put the omelette under it, then cook until the egg mixture bubbles up and turns golden brown. Serve the omelette freshly cooked, cut into wedges. **Serves 4**

Middle-Eastern Mince

(Illustrated on pages 66/67)

Lamb and goat are the meats which are eaten in the Middle East – pork is not eaten and the country is not conducive to rearing beef herds. When meat is eaten it is taken in small quantities and combined with vegetables and grains. Bread is served with most dishes and yogurt is also a frequent accompaniment. Okra, native to Africa and known in the Middle East as bamia, *is now widely available in this country. The ridged green pods are at their best when they are fairly small and tender; avoid the large pods which may be tough and stringy. It is important not to overcook okra as the pods have a tendency to become slimy. In this dish, lamb is very lightly spiced with coriander and nutmeg and cooked with tomatoes, then the whole okra pods are added for a few minutes before the lamb is served. A mixture of chick peas and sesame seeds and a bowl of yogurt accompany the meat mixture – bon appetit!*

225 g/8 oz dried chick peas
salt and freshly ground black
  pepper
225 g/8 oz small okra
1 red pepper
1 green pepper
1 large onion, peeled and
  chopped
2 tablespoons oil
1 large clove garlic, peeled and
  crushed
450 g/1 lb minced lamb

1 teaspoon ground coriander
1 teaspoon freshly grated
  nutmeg
2 (397-g/14-oz) cans chopped
  tomatoes
1 tablespoon chopped fresh
  mint
grated rind and juice of $\frac{1}{2}$ lemon
2 tablespoons sesame seeds
25 g/1 oz butter
150 ml/$\frac{1}{4}$ pint natural yogurt
warmed pitta bread to serve

Soak the chick peas overnight in plenty of cold water. Next day, drain them and cook them in lots of boiling, lightly salted water for about 45 minutes, or until just tender.

Trim the stalks off the okra, then wash each pod well, rubbing the skin with your finger. Cut the peppers in half, remove stalks, seeds and pith, chop the flesh and mix with the onion. Heat the oil in a flameproof casserole or heavy-based saucepan. Add the garlic, peppers and onion and cook until the onion is soft but not browned.

Add the lamb to the pan and fry it until it is lightly browned, breaking it up with a wooden spoon as it cooks. Stir in the coriander and nutmeg and plenty of seasoning then pour in the canned tomatoes. Bring to the boil, cover the pan and simmer gently for 20 minutes. Add the okra to the meat mixture, stir well and re-cover the pan, then continue to cook for a further 10 minutes, keeping the mixture just simmering all the time. If the mixture is cooking too rapidly, then the okra will be overcooked.

Strain the cooked chick peas and sprinkle the mint, lemon rind and juice and sesame seeds over them. Add the butter and toss well to mix the ingredients. Spread the chick peas in a large warmed serving dish.

Pour the yogurt into a small dish to serve with the lamb. Ladle the lamb over the chick peas, then serve at once, with the yogurt and warmed pitta bread. **Serves 4**

Veal in a Cream Sauce with Croûtons

Serve this simple but fairly rich mince dish with buttered noodles and Spinach and Bacon Salad (see page 173).

50 g/2 oz butter
1 large onion, chopped
675 g/1½ lb minced veal
2 tablespoons plain flour
salt and freshly ground black
   pepper
300 ml/½ pint dry white wine
blade of mace
bay leaf
sprig of thyme
225 g/8 oz button mushrooms,
   thinly sliced

150 ml/¼ pint soured cream
2 tablespoons chopped parsley
a little grated nutmeg
Croûtons
4 medium-thick slices bread,
   with crusts removed
25 g/1 oz butter
4 tablespoons oil
1 small clove garlic, peeled and
   crushed (optional)

Melt the butter in a flameproof casserole or heavy-based saucepan. Add the onion and cook, stirring frequently, until it is thoroughly softened but not brown. Stir in the veal and fry over a medium heat until it is just beginning to brown, stirring frequently to break it up and ensure that it cooks evenly. Stir in the flour and add seasoning to taste, then slowly pour in the wine, stirring all the time. Add the mace, bay leaf and thyme to the pan and bring to the boil. Reduce the heat, cover the pan and simmer gently for about 30 minutes.

While the meat is simmering, cook the croûtons. Cut the bread into small squares. Melt the butter with the oil in a frying pan. When the fat is hot add the garlic (if used) and cubes of bread and stir them round quickly so that they are evenly coated in fat. Fry the croûtons, stirring frequently to prevent them from overcooking on any one side, until they are golden all over. Drain on absorbent kitchen paper and set aside.

Remove the blade of mace, bay leaf and thyme from the mince then stir in the mushrooms and mix thoroughly over a moderate heat for 1 minute. Add the cream and parsley and heat through without boiling. Taste and adjust the seasoning as necessary, adding a little nutmeg. Serve at once, ladling the meat over cooked pasta, then top with the croûtons. **Serves 4**

Tipsy Lamb with Courgettes

(Illustrated opposite)

This is a simple dish of minced lamb cooked in wine (or stock if you prefer) with some mushrooms and celery, topped with lots of lightly fried courgettes. A touch of lemon juice on the vegetables counteracts the richness of the meat. Serve with minted new potatoes.

2 sticks of celery	2 tablespoons plain flour
50 g/2 oz butter	450 ml/$\frac{3}{4}$ pint red wine
1 onion, peeled, halved and thinly sliced	2 sprigs of rosemary
450 g/1 lb minced lamb	225 g/8 oz mushrooms, sliced
salt and freshly ground black pepper	350 g/12 oz courgettes
	a little lemon juice
	2 tablespoons chopped parsley

Trim the celery, cut the sticks lengthways into fine pieces, then cut these into 2.5-cm/1-in lengths. Put half the butter into a large frying pan or heavy-based saucepan and fry the celery with the onion. When the onion is just soft add the lamb and seasoning to taste, and continue to fry until the meat is lightly browned, stirring to break it up and ensure even cooking.

Stir in the flour and pour in the wine then add the rosemary and bring to the boil. Reduce the heat and simmer gently for 20 minutes. Stir in the mushrooms after 15 minutes. While the meat is simmering trim the ends off the courgettes and cut them into fine strips.

When the lamb is cooked melt the remaining butter in a separate pan then add the prepared courgettes and fry them quickly, stirring all the time, until they are very lightly cooked – this should take only a very few minutes. Sprinkle in seasoning to taste and a little lemon juice then add the parsley. Transfer the lamb to a serving dish and arrange the courgettes on top. Serve immediately. **Serves 4**

Opposite page *Top: Tipsy Lamb with Courgettes; Below: Lamb with Flageolet Beans (page 60)* **Overleaf** *Clockwise from top right: Middle Eastern Mince (page 62), Lamb with Kasha (page 69) and Spanish Pork with Orange (page 70)*

Lamb with Kasha

(Illustrated on pages 66/67))

Kasha is cracked wheat, available from health-food shops. Combined with meat, it gives a good texture, adding more bite to mince dishes, and it also gives the impression that there is more meat in the dish than there actually is. Serve a lively salad with this dish – you could try Avocado and Orange Salad or Spinach and Bacon Salad (see page 173), and offer some baked potatoes as well.

4 sticks of celery
1 large red or green pepper
2 tablespoons oil (groundnut oil would give an interesting flavour)
1 large onion, peeled and chopped
225 g/8 oz kasha

450 g/1 lb minced lamb
1 lamb or beef stock cube
450 ml/$\frac{3}{4}$ pint boiling water
salt and freshly ground black pepper
4 tablespoons chopped parsley
150 ml/$\frac{1}{4}$ pint soured cream or natural yogurt

Trim the celery, then cut the sticks in half lengthways and cut them across into chunks. Halve the pepper, remove the stalk, seeds and pith then chop the flesh. Heat the oil in a large frying pan which has a lid, a flameproof casserole or a heavy-based saucepan. Add the celery, pepper and onion and fry until the onion is soft but not browned. Add the kasha and cook for a few minutes, stirring all the time. Put the minced lamb in the pan and fry it, breaking it up as it cooks, until lightly browned.

Crumble the stock cube into the pan and pour the boiling water over it. Stir well, then bring the liquid back to the boil and reduce the heat so that it simmers gently. Cover the pan and cook for about 15 to 20 minutes. At the end of the cooking time most of the liquid should have been absorbed but the meat should still be juicy.

Stir in the parsley, swirl the soured cream or yogurt into the mixture and serve immediately. **Serves 4**

Top: Pork and Prawn Dim Sum (page 30); Below: Sweet and Sour Pork with Prawns (page 71)

Spanish Pork with Orange

(Illustrated on pages 66/67)

This simple dish of fried minced pork with peppers is enlivened by the addition of chorizos – spicy Spanish sausages – and some grated orange rind. Serve it with a bowl of buttered rice.

1 tablespoon oil
6 chorizos (about 450 g/1 lb), sliced
1 Spanish onion, peeled and sliced
1 large red pepper
1 large green pepper
450 g/1 lb minced pork

salt and freshly ground black pepper
grated rind and juice of 1 orange
1 (397-g/14-oz) can chopped tomatoes
150 ml/¼ pint Spanish red wine
2 large potatoes, cut into cubes

Heat the oil in a large frying pan which has a lid or in a flameproof casserole. Add the chorizos and fry them quickly until the cut ends are sealed. Use a draining spoon to remove them from the pan. Add the onion to the oil remaining in the pan. Cut the stalk ends off the peppers, remove the seeds and pith, slice the flesh and add to the pan with the onion. Fry until the vegetables are soft but not browned.

Stir the pork into the onion mixture and add seasoning to taste, then continue to cook until the meat is lightly browned. Stir in the orange rind and juice, the tomatoes and wine. Add the potatoes and bring to the boil. Cover the pan and simmer for 30 minutes. Finally, add the chorizos and heat for 2 minutes before serving. **Serves 4**

Pork and Potato Hash

This is one of those recipes that is satisfyingly tasty – good bed-sit food or cheap and cheerful family fare. If you want to prepare a particularly substantial meal, then offer something like a cauliflower au gratin with this hash.

1 large onion, peeled and finely chopped
50 g/2 oz butter
100 g/4 oz carrots, coarsely grated
450 g/1 lb potatoes, coarsely grated

450 g/1 lb minced pork
1 egg, beaten
salt and freshly ground black pepper
4 tablespoons chopped parsley
100 g/4 oz mushrooms, chopped
50 g/2 oz fresh breadcrumbs

Fry the onion in the butter until it is soft but not browned. Add the carrots and potatoes and stir quickly, then cook for a few minutes. Remove the pan from the heat to add the meat, stirring it in well to break it up and mix it evenly with the vegetables. With the pan still off the heat, stir in the beaten egg and plenty of seasoning, then add the parsley and mushrooms. Mix in the breadcrumbs and press the mixture flat in the pan, smoothing the top over.

Return the pan to the heat, keeping it fairly low, and cook gently for about 20 to 30 minutes, until the base of the hash is well browned. Then put the pan under a hot grill and cook until browned all over. The grill should be set at a moderate heat so that the meat and vegetables cook evenly and not too quickly. Serve the hash cut into wedges with a chutney – why not try peach chutney? It tastes very good. **Serves 4**

Sweet and Sour Pork with Prawns

(Illustrated on page 68)

Cook some plain rice to go with this dish. To make an interesting Oriental meal you could prepare Spring Rolls (see page 24) as the first course.

450 g/1 lb minced pork
a few drops of sesame oil
1 (227-g/8-oz) can water
　chestnuts
1 (227-g/8-oz) can pineapple
　slices in natural juice
2 tablespoons soy sauce

4 tablespoons tomato ketchup
1 tablespoon dark brown sugar
1 bunch spring onions, chopped
100 g/4 oz peeled cooked prawns
2 teaspoons cornflour
4 tablespoons dry sherry

Put the pork in a frying pan with the sesame oil and heat slowly until the fat runs. Fry the pork until lightly browned.

Meanwhile, drain the water chestnuts and slice them. Drain the pineapple, reserve the juice and cut the fruit into small pieces. Add the fruit and the juice to the meat then stir in the soy sauce, ketchup and sugar. Add the onions to the pan and bring to the boil. Stir in the prawns, return to the boil and simmer gently for a few minutes.

Blend the cornflour with the sherry, then pour this into the pan and simmer for 3 to 4 minutes or until the mixture has thoroughly thickened. Serve at once, transferred into one large serving dish ready to eat from small bowls with chopsticks. **Serves 4**

BAKED IN THE OVEN

Hearty hot pots, traditional cottage pie, cobblers and meat loaves are all included here, but spicy recipes and more sophisticated ideas are also featured so that there are ideas for every type of meal from those boring day-to-day menus to those for informal friendly entertaining.

Cottage Pie

There are cottage pies and cottage pies; some good, others very poor indeed. I like cottage pie which has a nice juicy meat base, with mushrooms and plenty of flavour, and a good potato topping – enough to completely seal in the base so that it doesn't ooze out to make the potato soggy. Then to finish it off the top should be nicely browned and crusty.

1 large onion, peeled and chopped	225 g/8 oz mushrooms, sliced
50 g/2 oz butter	salt and freshly ground black pepper
675 g/1½ lb minced beef	*Topping*
2 tablespoons plain flour	1.5 kg/3 lb potatoes
1 beef stock cube	salt and freshly ground black pepper
generous dash of Worcestershire sauce	milk and butter for mashing, plus extra butter for baking
bay leaf	
600 ml/1 pint water	

Fry the onion in the butter until soft but not browned. Add the beef and cook, breaking up the meat, until lightly browned. Stir in the flour, crumble in the stock cube, add the Worcestershire sauce and bay leaf. Pour in the water, stirring all the time, then bring to the boil. Reduce the heat and cover the pan then simmer gently for 30 minutes.

Meanwhile prepare the potato topping. Cook the potatoes in boiling salted water for about 20 minutes or until tender. Drain and thoroughly mash them, making sure they are smooth. Beat in plenty of milk and butter and a good sprinkling of freshly ground black pepper. The potatoes must be moist enough to spread over the meat but not too soft.

Add the mushrooms to the mince mixture and adjust the seasoning to your taste, then turn the meat into a large ovenproof dish. Spread the potatoes over the top making sure they go right up to the edge of the dish. Mark the top deeply with a fork and dot with butter. Bake in a moderately hot oven (200 C, 400 F, gas 6) for 30 to 40 minutes or until brown and crisp on top. Serve freshly cooked. **Serves 4 to 6**

Savoury Charlotte

This is both inexpensive and delicious. Serve the charlotte with a m
vegetable dish to make a satisfying meal – a good cauliflower au gratin
with plenty of sauce would go very well indeed. Cook a cauliflower in
boiling water for 10 minutes, then drain it thoroughly, leaving it draining
while you make Cheese Sauce (see page 162). Put the cauliflower in an
ovenproof dish and pour the sauce over. Sprinkle a little grated cheese and
some breadcrumbs on top. Have this ready to go in the oven for the last 20
to 30 minutes cooking time for the charlotte.

1 large onion, peeled and
  chopped
2 tablespoons oil
450 g/1 lb minced beef
$\frac{1}{2}$ teaspoon thyme
$\frac{1}{2}$ teaspoon rubbed sage
$\frac{1}{2}$ teaspoon ground mixed spice
2 tablespoons concentrated
  tomato purée

salt and freshly ground black
  pepper
75–100 g/3–4 oz butter or
  margarine
7–8 slices fresh bread
2 eggs
300 ml/$\frac{1}{2}$ pint milk

Fry the onion in the oil in a large frying pan until soft but not browned.
Add the minced beef, breaking it up with a wooden spoon, then cook
until browned. Stir in the herbs and spice, tomato purée and seasoning
to taste. Remove from the heat and set aside.

Butter the bread (remove the crusts first if you like but there is no
real need to do so) then use the slices to line a 1.15-litre/2-pint
ovenproof dish, with the buttered side on the outside. Reserve a few
slices of bread for covering the top. Spoon the mince mixture into the
dish, but do not press it down. Lay the reserved slices of bread on top,
with the buttered sides up. You may have to cut the bread up to cover
the top neatly.

Beat the eggs, then beat in the milk and add seasoning to taste.
Slowly pour this mixture over the bread, allowing time for it to soak in.
Bake in a moderately hot oven (200 C, 400 F, gas 6) for 45 minutes, until
golden brown. Serve at once. **Serves 4**

Note. If you do not plan to serve a moist vegetable dish with the
charlotte, then you may like to prepare a sauce to accompany it. Try,
for example, the Cheese Sauce or the Mushroom Sauce (both on page
162) or why not make the Rich Tomato Sauce on page 163?

Beef and Cabbage Cobbler

(Illustrated on page 85)

This wholesome mixture of meat and vegetables topped with cheese-flavoured scones makes a satisfying meal in itself. If you expect the family to be really hungry, then double the quantity of scone topping mixture.

2 tablespoons oil
1 large onion, peeled and
  chopped
450 g/1 lb minced beef
1 tablespoon fennel seeds or
  caraway seeds
salt and freshly ground black
  pepper
100 g/4 oz carrots, cut into thin
  strips
100 g/4 oz button mushrooms,
  sliced

600 ml/1 pint pale ale
1 beef stock cube
450 g/1 lb white cabbage,
  shredded
Scone topping
100 g/4 oz self-raising flour, plus
  a little for rolling out
a pinch of salt
25 g/1 oz butter
25 ml/$2\frac{1}{2}$ fl oz milk
25 g/1 oz matured Cheddar
  cheese, grated

Heat the oil in a large saucepan, then add the onion and fry until soft but not browned. Add the minced beef and cook, breaking up the meat with a wooden spoon, until evenly browned. Stir in the fennel or caraway seeds and cook for 2 minutes then add seasoning to taste and the vegetables. Pour in the ale and crumble in the stock cube then bring to the boil. Lastly stir in the cabbage and bring back to the boil. Remove the pan from the heat and transfer the mixture to an ovenproof dish.

For the topping, sift the flour into a bowl and add a pinch of salt. Rub in the butter until the mixture resembles fine breadcrumbs, then stir in the milk to make a soft mixture (it should be softer than a normal scone dough). Divide it roughly into six portions and roll each portion in a little flour. Flatten each piece of dough slightly then place them on top of the beef mixture. Sprinkle the cheese over the scones and bake in a hot oven (220 C, 425 F, gas 7) for 25 minutes or until the scones are risen and golden. Serve immediately. **Serves 4**

Beef Gougère

(Illustrated on page 85)

A gougère is made of choux pastry, with the pastry piped or spooned into a circle in an ovenproof dish. The filling is turned into the ring, then the whole is baked. A combination of a few very simple ingredients turned out to be quite delicious in this gougère. It makes an excellent supper dish which requires no other accompaniment.

1 large onion, peeled and chopped
2 tablespoons oil
450 g/1 lb minced beef
100 g/4 oz button mushrooms, sliced
salt and freshly ground black pepper
1 (397-g/14-oz) can chopped tomatoes
Choux pastry
150 ml/$\frac{1}{4}$ pint water

65 g/2$\frac{1}{2}$ oz butter
65 g/2$\frac{1}{2}$ oz plain flour
2 eggs
100 g/4 oz mature Cheddar cheese, grated
Topping
100 g/4 oz rindless streaky bacon
25 g/1 oz Cheddar cheese, grated
25 g/1 oz fresh breadcrumbs

Fry the onion in the oil until soft but not browned. Add the mince and cook, breaking it up as it cooks, until evenly browned. Stir in the mushrooms and cook for a few minutes, then stir in seasoning to taste and pour in the tomatoes. Bring to the boil then remove from the heat and set aside.

Pour the water for the choux pastry into a saucepan. Add the butter and heat gently until the butter melts, then bring to the boil. As soon as the mixture boils, remove the pan from the heat and add all the flour. Beat it in well but do not overmix it; the mixture should come away from the sides of the saucepan in one lump. Allow to cool for a few minutes. Lightly beat the eggs, then beat them vigorously into the flour and water paste. Continue beating until the paste is smooth and very glossy. Beat in the grated cheese and seasoning.

Grease a 25-cm/10-in ovenproof dish – the best to use would be a fairly deep gratin dish or deep quiche dish. Spoon the paste round the edge of the dish, making it as even as possible and piling it up slightly. Pile the minced beef mixture into the middle of the ring.

For the topping, roughly chop the bacon, then mix it with the cheese and the breadcrumbs. Pile this over the beef and bake the gougère in a hot oven (220 C, 425 F, gas 7) for 45 minutes, or until the choux pastry is well risen and golden brown. When cut the pastry will be deliciously moist in the middle. Serve at once. **Serves 4**

Ring of Beef with Ham

(Illustrated on pages 86/87)

This dish just goes to show how mince can be turned into something quite special: all it takes is a little imagination!

675 g/1½ lb minced beef
1 onion, peeled and finely
  chopped
1 teaspoon thyme
1 teaspoon marjoram
2 teaspoons Dijon mustard
1 clove garlic, peeled and
  crushed
1 egg, beaten
salt and freshly ground black
  pepper
175 g/6 oz carrots, sliced
50 g/2 oz butter

50 g/2 oz dried apricots,
  chopped (use the type which
  do not require pre-soaking)
50 g/2 oz fresh breadcrumbs
1–2 tablespoons orange juice
275 g/10 oz sliced cooked ham
To serve
1 small head endive
1 bunch spring onions, chopped
½ cucumber, peeled and
  chopped
2 tablespoons olive oil
2 tablespoons lemon juice

Mix the beef with the onion, herbs, mustard, garlic and egg. Add plenty of seasoning, then give the mixture a good stir to make sure that all the ingredients are thoroughly combined. Set aside.

Cook the carrots in boiling salted water until tender – about 15 minutes. Drain and mash with the butter. Beat in the apricots and breadcrumbs with enough orange juice to moisten the mixture.

Thoroughly grease a 1.15-litre/2-pint ring tin then line it neatly with the sliced ham. Press the meat mixture into the tin, leaving a hollow all the way round to put the carrot stuffing in. You should use about two-thirds of the meat for this. Put the carrot and apricot stuffing neatly into the middle of the meat, pressing it down well to leave room for the last of the meat to go on top. Put the remaining meat in the tin to cover the stuffing completely. Fold the ends of the ham over the meat – you will have to snip into the pieces on the inner side of the ring. Wrap the ring in cooking foil and bake it in a moderate oven (180 C, 350 F, gas 5) for 1 hour.

Prepare the endive salad while the meat is cooking. Trim and wash the endive and shred it finely. Mix it with the spring onions and cucumber, then toss in the oil and lemon juice and add seasoning.

To serve, turn the ring out on to a heatproof platter and put the salad in the middle. Cut the ring into slices and the stuffing will look most attractive. **Serves 6**

Stuffed Aubergines with Cucumber Sauce

A filling of lamb, scented with rosemary and lemon, turns two large aubergines into a quite special main course for four, with a light cucumber sauce to complete the otherwise rich main dish. Serve buttered pasta and a simple salad, French beans or courgettes to accompany the aubergines.

2 large aubergines
salt and freshly ground black
  pepper
1 large onion, peeled and finely
  chopped
450 g/1 lb minced lamb
grated rind of 1 lemon
1 tablespoon chopped fresh
  rosemary
150 ml/$\frac{1}{4}$ pint red wine

100 g/4 oz feta cheese
Cucumber sauce
1 small cucumber
150 ml/$\frac{1}{4}$ pint soured cream
a little freshly grated nutmeg
2 tablespoons chopped parsley
Garnish
4 slices of lemon, halved
4 rosemary sprigs

Cut the aubergines in half lengthways. Using a small pointed knife, cut through the flesh in a criss-cross pattern, being careful not to damage the skins, then use a teaspoon to scoop out all the cut-up flesh. Chop this finely and place it in a colander or sieve, sprinkle with salt and set aside for 30 minutes.

Place the onion in a large frying pan with the lamb and heat gently for a few minutes then fry until the onion is soft and the lamb is browned. Stir the meat as it cooks to break it up and make sure it cooks evenly. Add the lemon rind and rosemary to the pan, stir in seasoning to taste and pour in the wine. Bring to the boil then remove from the heat.

Rinse the aubergine, squeeze out all the water then add it to the meat mixture. Spoon the mixture back into the aubergine shells and place them in a greased ovenproof dish. Crumble the feta cheese, sprinkle it evenly over the aubergines and cook them in a moderately hot oven (190 C, 375 F, gas 5) for about 45 minutes until golden brown on top.

While the aubergines are cooking prepare the sauce. Trim and lightly peel the cucumber, grate it finely, place it in a colander or sieve and sprinkle with a little salt. Set aside for 30 minutes, then squeeze out all the liquid, place the cucumber in a bowl and pour in the soured cream. Add nutmeg to taste and stir in the parsley. Chill lightly until you are ready to serve the aubergines.

Before serving, garnish each aubergine half with some lemon and a sprig of rosemary if you like. Offer the cucumber sauce separately.
Serves 4

Stuffed Cabbage with Stilton Cream

The addition of a slightly unusual hot or cold sauce or dressing often turns a familiar recipe into an interesting and quite new one. I have prepared a creamy Stilton mixture to complement this stuffed cabbage but you could equally well serve a hot sauce with it. For example, why not try Red Wine Sauce (page 164), Mushroom Sauce (page 162) or Devilled Mayonnaise (page 170) instead?

1 Savoy cabbage (about 1.25–1.5 kg/2½–3 lb)
2 tablespoons oil
1 large onion, peeled and chopped
50 g/2 oz walnuts, chopped
1 piece preserved stem ginger
450 g/1 lb minced beef
salt and freshly ground black pepper
grated rind and juice of 1 orange

1 (439-g/15.5-oz) can butter beans, drained
2 tablespoons chopped parsley
25 g/1 oz butter
Stilton cream
175 g/6 oz ripe Stilton cheese
150 ml/¼ pint single cream
2 spring onions, finely chopped
dash of lemon juice

Select a firm round cabbage without too many large loose outer leaves. Trim off any damaged leaves and cut a piece from the base so that the cabbage sits neatly upright. Slice the top off then make criss-cross cuts down into the middle and remove the cut cabbage to leave a shell about three or four leaves thick. Cut away as much of the tough inner stalk as you can, leaving just enough to hold the shell together. Reserve the cut-away cabbage for another day (it will keep well in a polythene bag in the bottom of the refrigerator), or alternatively sauté the shreds in a little butter and season them to serve with the cooked stuffed cabbage.

Heat the oil in a frying pan and add the onion. Fry, stirring frequently, until the onion is just soft, then add the walnuts and continue to cook for a few minutes. Thoroughly drain the ginger of any syrup, then chop it finely and add it to the onion mixture. Stir in the minced beef and add seasoning to taste. Fry the meat until lightly cooked then stir in the orange rind and juice, butter beans and parsley. Remove from the heat.

Stand the cabbage on a very large piece of cooking foil in a roasting tin or ovenproof dish. Spoon the meat mixture into the cabbage shell, pressing it down well if necessary so that it will all fit in. Top with the butter then fold the foil securely around the cabbage to enclose it completely and keep in all the juices during cooking. Bake in a moderately hot oven (200 C, 400 F, gas 6) for 1½ hours.

To make the Stilton cream, crumble the cheese into a basin, then mix in the cream. Use a fork to break up the cheese – the sauce should not be smooth but the cheese must be broken sufficiently to thicken and thoroughly flavour the cream. Add the spring onions and lemon juice, then season with freshly ground black pepper to taste. Chill thoroughly before serving.

Lift the cooked cabbage on to a warmed serving dish and pour the cooking juices from the foil over the filling. Serve at once, cutting the cabbage into wedges at the table. Hand the Stilton cream separately.
Serves 4 to 6

Gratin of Stuffed Peppers

This is an interesting way to treat stuffed peppers – fill them with the usual sort of meaty mixture (here, pork and beef combined with cheese and peanuts), then lay them in a dish and sprinkle over a topping which will become crisp on baking. Serve a moist, mayonnaise-dressed salad with the peppers; and cook some baked potatoes too.

4 long green peppers
225 g/8 oz minced pork
225 g/8 oz minced beef
1 small onion, peeled and finely chopped or grated
100 g/4 oz matured Cheddar cheese, grated
100 g/4 oz unroasted peanuts, ground to a powder (do this in a liquidiser or food processor, or use a mouli grater)

2 tablespoons tomato ketchup
salt and freshly ground black pepper
chopped parsley to garnish
Topping
1 bag salted crisps, crushed
50 g/2 oz Cheddar cheese, grated

Cut the stalk ends off the peppers then remove all the seeds and pith from inside. Cook the peppers in a large saucepan of boiling water for 2 minutes then drain thoroughly in a colander. If you do not have a very large saucepan you may have to cook the peppers two-by-two, in which case use a draining spoon to lift them out of the cooking water rather than boiling two lots. Lay the drained peppers on a double thickness of absorbent kitchen paper to dry.

Mix the meats with the onion, cheese and peanuts then add the ketchup and seasoning to taste. When all the ingredients are thoroughly combined, divide the mixture into four equal portions and stuff one into each of the peppers. Lay the stuffed peppers in a greased ovenproof dish.

Mix the crisps and the cheese for the topping then sprinkle the mixture down the middle of the peppers. Cover with cooking foil and bake in a moderately hot oven (200 C, 400 F, gas 6) for 30 minutes. Uncover the dish and cook for a further 10 minutes. Serve at once.
Serves 4

Stuffed Courgettes

These make an excellent main course, but you could also halve the quantities and serve them as a starter.

450 g/1 lb minced beef
3 teaspoons celery seeds
2 tablespoons concentrated
    tomato purée
salt and freshly ground black
    pepper
1 onion, peeled and finely
    chopped

1 tablespoon oil
4 large courgettes
16 rashers rindless streaky
    bacon
8 bay leaves
sprigs of watercress to garnish

Put the beef in a bowl and add the celery seeds, tomato purée and seasoning to taste. Fry the onion in the oil until it is soft but not browned then add it to the meat and mix thoroughly.

Cut the courgettes in half lengthways then scoop out and discard all the seeds. Fill the courgette halves with the meat mixture, moulding it neatly on to each piece. Lay a bay leaf on each stuffed courgette then wrap two rashers of bacon around each. Place in an ovenproof dish and bake in a hot oven (220 C, 425 F, gas 7) for 30 minutes. Serve the courgettes immediately they are cooked, adding a few sprigs of watercress to each piece. **Serves 4**

Curried Beef with Aubergines

Serve this spicy mixture with cooked basmati rice and some mango pickle. Offer crisp popadums with the curry.

2 aubergines
salt and freshly ground black
    pepper
2 green chillies
3 cloves
3 green cardamoms
1 tablespoon cumin seeds
4 tablespoons oil
1 large onion, peeled and
    chopped

1 cinnamon stick
2 cloves garlic, peeled and
    crushed
2 teaspoons ground ginger
450 g/1 lb minced beef
1 (397-g/14-oz) can chopped
    tomatoes
1 beef stock cube
300 ml/$\frac{1}{2}$ pint water
150 ml/$\frac{1}{4}$ pint natural yogurt

Cut the stalk end off the aubergines then cut the rest into cubes and place them in a colander or sieve over a bowl. Sprinkle generously with salt and set aside. The salt will draw out the juices which can make the aubergines taste bitter when they are cooked.

Cut off and discard the stalk ends from the chillies and remove all the seeds from inside. Take care if you are not used to handling chillies – do not rub your eyes as the merest hint of chilli juice will sting dreadfully. The seeds are the hottest part of the chilli and they should all be removed. This done, chop the green part finely. Grind the cloves with the cardamoms and cumin seeds to a coarse powder, using a pestle and mortar, liquidiser, food processor or coffee grinder.

Heat the oil in a heavy-based saucepan or flameproof casserole, add the onion and chillies with the cinnamon stick and garlic and fry until the onion is soft but not browned. Stir in the ground spices, ginger and beef and fry until the beef is all broken up.

Thoroughly rinse then dry the aubergines and add them to the pan. Continue cooking, turning frequently until they are evenly and lightly cooked. Add seasoning to taste, then the tomatoes. Crumble in the stock cube, pour in the water and the yogurt and bring to the boil. Reduce the heat and simmer, uncovered, for about 30 minutes or until most of the liquid has evaporated to leave a juicy meat and aubergine mixture. Sprinkle the chopped coriander over and serve at once. **Serves 4**

Lancashire-style Leeks with Lamb

This tasty minced lamb dish makes a meal in itself – it's good traditional-type fare for when you're feeling cold and hungry.

4 leeks
225 g/8 oz carrots
2 tablespoons oil
675 g/1½ lb minced lamb
salt and freshly ground black
   pepper
2 tablespoons plain flour

1 lamb or chicken stock cube
600 ml/1 pint water
bay leaf
generous dash of Worcestershire
   sauce
1 kg/2 lb potatoes
a little butter

The vegetables for this dish should be fairly chunky. Slice and thoroughly wash the leeks and drain them well. Slice the carrots. Heat the oil in a large frying pan or heavy-based saucepan, add the vegetables and fry for a few minutes, then stir in the lamb and season to taste. Break up the meat as it cooks and fry until lightly browned. Stir in the flour and crumbled stock cube then pour in the water, add the bay leaf and Worcestershire sauce. Bring to the boil briefly then transfer to a large ovenproof dish or casserole.

Slice the potatoes fairly thickly and lay them overlapping each other on top of the meat mixture. Dot with butter, cover with foil then bake in a moderately hot oven (200 C, 400 F, gas 6) for 30 minutes. Remove the foil covering and bake for a further 45 minutes or until the vegetables are tender and browned on top. Serve at once. **Serves 4**

Veal and Olive Loaf

(Illustrated on pages 86/87)

This is the sort of meat loaf that would make a good main dish for an informal dinner party – it's interestingly different, very well flavoured and if you use your imagination when it comes to garnishing, then it can also look good. However, it is worth checking that your guests eat veal, as some people avoid it.

175 g/6 oz lean rindless bacon
450 g/1 lb minced veal
1 small onion, peeled and finely
  chopped
100 g/4 oz green olives, stoned
75 g/3 oz fresh breadcrumbs
2 teaspoons dried basil

4 tablespoons dry sherry
1 egg, beaten
salt and freshly ground black
  pepper
Garnish
2 tomatoes, cut into wedges
sprigs of watercress

Chop the bacon, removing any small bones, and mix it with the veal. Add all the remaining ingredients and mix them together thoroughly so that they are well combined and evenly distributed.

Line the base of a 450-g/1-lb loaf tin with a piece of greaseproof paper (there is no need to do this if you know that your tin will not stick but it is a good idea if you have any doubts). Grease the tin fairly thoroughly then press the meat mixture into it and smooth the top with the back of a metal spoon. Stand the tin on a Swiss roll tin or similar to catch any juices which may overflow from the meat loaf and bake in a moderate oven (180 C, 350 F, gas 4) for 1 hour.

Pour off the juices from the cooked meat loaf then turn it out on to a serving platter. Use the juices to flavour a sauce – try making White Wine Sauce or Tomato Sauce (see pages 164 and 163) – which can be served with the meat loaf. Add the garnishing ingredients to the platter and serve at once. The meat loaf can also be allowed to cool in the tin and can then be served cold. **Serves 4**

Moussaka

Serve this delicious Greek dish with a crisp, fresh green salad. Make a light oil and vinegar dressing then sprinkle a few toasted sesame seeds over the salad after the dressing is poured on. Offer some crusty bread with the moussaka.

450 g/1 lb aubergines
olive oil for cooking
1 large onion, peeled and
 chopped
3 cloves garlic, peeled and
 crushed
450 g/1 lb minced lamb
2 teaspoons marjoram
salt and freshly ground black
 pepper
2 tablespoons plain flour

1 (397-g/14-oz) can chopped
 tomatoes
150 ml/$\frac{1}{4}$ pint red vermouth or
 full-bodied red wine
Topping
50 g/2 oz self-raising flour
3 eggs
150 ml/$\frac{1}{4}$ pint natural yogurt
50 g/2 oz Cheddar cheese, grated
 (optional)

Trim the ends off the aubergines, slice them and place the slices in a colander. Sprinkle them fairly generously with salt and set aside over a plate or bowl for 30 minutes. The salt will draw out the excess juices, which can taste bitter when cooked.

Meanwhile, pour a little oil into a large frying pan and cook the onion and garlic until the onion is soft but not browned. Stir in the lamb and continue to fry, breaking up the meat as it cooks, until lightly browned. Stir in the marjoram and seasoning to taste, then sprinkle the flour over the meat and stir well. Pour in the tomatoes and vermouth or wine. Bring to the boil and remove from the heat. Set aside.

Thoroughly rinse and drain the aubergines. Heat a little olive oil in a large frying pan and add a few slices of aubergine. Cook until browned on the underside then turn and cook the other side. Remove from the pan, drain on absorbent kitchen paper, and continue frying batches, working fairly quickly so that the slices brown before becoming too soft. Aubergines absorb quite a lot of oil, so you will have to add more as you go along.

Layer the aubergine slices and meat in a large ovenproof dish, beginning and ending with a layer of aubergines. For the topping sift the flour into a bowl and add a little salt. Gradually beat in the eggs, then the yogurt. Pour this evenly over the moussaka and sprinkle with the cheese, if used. Bake in a moderately hot oven (200 C, 400 F, gas 6) for about 45 to 50 minutes, or until the topping is well risen, crisp and golden brown. Serve immediately. **Serves 4**

Note. If you do not like the flavour of olive oil or feel that it is too expensive to use in this way, then try corn oil or a similar light oil.

Baked Spiced Lamb

This is a very simple Indian-style recipe. Serve it with some cooked basmati rice and White Radish Raita (below).

40 g/1½ oz fresh root ginger
1 onion, peeled and finely
   chopped
450 g/1 lb minced lamb
1 tablespoon ground coriander
1 tablespoon ground fenugreek
1 teaspoon chilli powder

1 teaspoon turmeric
salt and freshly ground black
   pepper
Garnish
2 hard-boiled eggs, cut into
   wedges
1 lemon, cut into wedges

Grate the root ginger – there is no need to peel it first, but discard the very last bit which will be mostly peel and a few stringy bits of ginger. Mix the ginger with the onion and lamb in a bowl and add all the remaining ingredients, mixing well.

Press the mixture into a 23-cm/9-in sandwich tin and bake in a moderately hot oven (200 C, 400 F, gas 6) for 30 minutes. Turn the cooked meat out on to a serving platter and cut it into wedges. Separate the wedges slightly, then garnish with the hard-boiled eggs and lemon wedges and serve immediately. **Serves 4**

White Radish Raita

Take one large white radish (also known as a *mooli*) and peel and grate it coarsely. Place the grated radish in a sieve and sprinkle with a little salt. Set aside for 30 minutes, then squeeze all the liquid out of the radish and place it in a dish. Add 1 tablespoon chopped fresh coriander leaves, then stir in 4 tablespoons well chilled natural yogurt. Sprinkle a little ground coriander on top and serve.

Opposite page *Top: Beef Gougère (page 75); Below: Beef and Cabbage Cobbler (page 74)* **Overleaf** *From left to right: Ring of Beef with Ham (page 76), Pork and Spinach Roulade (page 92) and Veal and Olive Loaf (page 82)*

Savoury Oranges

(Illustrated opposite)

Scooped-out orange shells make interesting vessels for a savoury minced pork mixture, at the same time the tangy orange peel adds zest to the meat. Serve the oranges with a crisp green salad (see page 172) and sautéed potatoes.

50 g/2 oz long-grain rice
150 ml/$\frac{1}{4}$ pint water
salt and freshly ground black
   pepper
4 large oranges
2 tablespoons crunchy peanut
   butter

1 leek, washed, trimmed and
   finely chopped
1 teaspoon chilli powder
   (optional)
450 g/1 lb minced pork

Put the rice in a saucepan, pour in the water, add a little salt and bring to the boil. Cover the pan, reduce the heat and simmer gently for about 15 minutes or until the rice has absorbed all the water.

Meanwhile, cut just the very top off each orange and carefully squeeze the juice from the fruit, being sure not to break the skins. Scoop out all the remaining flesh and pips with a teaspoon and discard them. Reserve the juice.

Add the peanut butter and leek to the freshly cooked rice and stir well. Mix in the chilli powder (if used) and pork, making sure all the ingredients are well combined. Add seasoning to taste and 4 tablespoons of the orange juice (chill the rest to drink). Fill the orange shells with the meat mixture and wrap each one completely in cooking foil. Stand the packages in an ovenproof dish and bake in a moderately hot oven (200 C, 400 F, gas 6) for 40 minutes then open the tops of the packages and cook for a further 10 to 15 minutes. Serve hot, arranging them on one large serving platter or on individual plates. **Serves 4**

Top: Savoury Oranges; Below: Stuffed Cabbage Leaves with Potato Dice (page 94)

Spicy Lamb and Potato Loaf

Serve this slightly curried loaf with basmati rice and a moist vegetable dish – try a mixture of lightly fried aubergines with canned tomatoes, for example. The Cucumber Raita (below) should be served separately to accompany the sliced loaf.

2 leeks (about 275–350 g/10–12 oz in weight)
450 g/1 lb potatoes
3 tablespoons grated fresh root ginger
450 g/1 lb minced lamb
2 eggs
1 tablespoon ground coriander
2 cloves garlic, peeled and crushed
1 teaspoon ground cumin
salt and freshly ground black pepper
4 tablespoons chopped fresh coriander leaves

Trim the leeks then quarter them lengthways and cut them across into small pieces. Wash and drain thoroughly. Peel and grate the potatoes. Mix these with all the other ingredients in a large bowl, stirring thoroughly to make sure that the mince is well broken up and evenly combined with the vegetables. Grease a 1-kg/2-lb loaf tin and line the base with a piece of greaseproof paper. Grease the paper well, then turn the mixture into the tin and smooth the top. Cover the loaf with cooking foil and cook in a moderately hot oven (200 C, 400 F, gas 6) for 1 hour. Turn out and serve hot. **Serves 4 to 6**

Cucumber Raita
Peel and dice 1 medium cucumber. Place the pieces in a colander and sprinkle with salt, then set aside over a bowl for 30 minutes. Shake the colander to remove the drops of liquid which will have formed on the pieces of cucumber, then dry thoroughly on several thicknesses of absorbent kitchen paper. Place in a serving bowl, pour in 150 ml/$\frac{1}{4}$ pint well-chilled natural yogurt, mix well and sprinkle a little chilli powder over the surface of the raita. Serve at once. If the cucumber is allowed to stand for too long it will weep and thin down the yogurt.

Bobotie

Fruity lamb with curry spices forms the base for this dish which is then topped with a savoury custard mixture and baked until set and golden. It goes very well with salad – a simple green salad would be quite adequate, or try one of those on page 173 – and some buttered basmati rice.

1 large onion, peeled and chopped

2 cloves garlic, peeled and crushed

2 tablespoons oil

1 cinnamon stick

4 teaspoons ground cumin

4 teaspoons ground coriander

3 green cardamoms

2 tablespoons grated fresh root ginger

675 g/1½ lb minced lamb

salt and freshly ground black pepper

50 g/2 oz raisins

50 g/2 oz dried apricots (the type which do not need pre-soaking), chopped

300 ml/½ pint water

Topping

50 g/2 oz plain flour

salt

2 eggs

300 ml/½ pint milk

Fry the onion and garlic in the oil until the onion is soft but not browned. Add all the spices and the root ginger and cook for 2 to 3 minutes, stirring continuously. Add the lamb and break it up with a wooden spoon, stir in seasoning to taste and continue to cook until the meat is lightly browned. Stir in the fruit and pour in the water, then bring to the boil and simmer steadily, uncovered, for 5 minutes. The mixture should be very moist but not too runny at the end of the cooking time. If there is a lot of water left then boil very fast for a minute or so to reduce it. Transfer to an ovenproof dish – about 1.4 litres/2½ pints in capacity.

Sift the flour for the topping into a bowl. Add a generous pinch of salt and beat in the eggs, gradually adding the milk to make a smooth batter. Press the surface of the meat mixture down well, then pour over the topping and bake in a moderately hot oven (200 C, 400 F, gas 6) for 50 to 60 minutes or until golden brown and set on top. Serve at once.
Serves 4

Cooking Basmati Rice
Basmati rice is Indian rice which has a fine flavour and a delicate fragrance. Before cooking the grains should be washed in several changes of water then drained thoroughly. Be careful not to damage the rice by stirring it vigorously or it will become sticky. Once washed the rice can be cooked as for any long-grain variety, although more care is necessary than for the easy-cook varieties.

Pork and Spinach Roulade

(Illustrated on pages 86/87 and front cover)

Serve this meat roll either hot with Tomato and Celery Sauce (see page 163) or cold with Herb Mayonnaise (see page 170). Keep the accompaniments simple – buttered new potatoes or a plain baked potato dish and some glazed carrots or lightly cooked courgettes. A crisp green salad with lots of avocado and spring onions would go very well with the cold roulade. The uncooked or prepared roulade can be frozen successfully for up to 3 or 4 months.

2 (227-g/8-oz) frozen leaf spinach	salt and freshly ground black pepper
1 kg/2 lb minced pork	225 g/8 oz Ricotta cheese
1 large clove garlic, peeled and crushed	2 teaspoons chopped chives
4 tablespoons brandy	freshly grated nutmeg

Defrost the spinach then drain it thoroughly and squeeze out the leaves to remove all excess moisture.

Place the meat in a basin and thoroughly mix in the garlic, brandy, and a generous amount of seasoning. Cut a large piece of cooking foil – unless it is very strong foil make it double – and lay it on a flat surface. Grease the foil lightly then turn the pork mixture out on to it. Use your hands to shape the meat into an oblong measuring about 23 × 25 cm/ 9 × 10 in. Knead the meat together thoroughly as you shape it so that it binds together well. The meat should be fairly even in thickness, with nicely squared corners.

Mix the cheese with the chives, a generous sprinkling of nutmeg and just a little seasoning, breaking the cheese up evenly. Lay the spinach over the meat, leaving a narrow border round the edge. Put the cheese down the middle then lift the foil at one of the short edges and carefully fold the meat over so that it lies down the middle of the filling. Peel back the foil. Lift the opposite side over to enclose the cheese and spinach completely. Pinch the meat together thoroughly down the join then smooth it over with your fingers to make sure that it is well sealed together. Pinch the opposite ends together to enclose the filling, then fold the foil tightly around the meat, rolling the edges to seal the package. Gently roll the package to form a neat shape, then place it on a baking tray or roasting tin and cook in a moderately hot oven (200 C, 400 F, gas 6) for 1¼ to 1½ hours.

To serve, carefully open the foil and slice the meat roll – a sharp serrated knife is best for this. Lay the slices, overlapping them neatly, on a warmed serving platter and add any meat juices to a sauce if you have prepared one. To serve the roulade cold, leave it tightly wrapped in the foil until cool, then chill it lightly and slice to serve. **Serves 4 to 6**

Pork and Parsnip Bake

Serve baked or sautéed potatoes to accompany this flavoursome savoury bake. The dish can be prepared in advance and frozen for several months, ready to defrost and brown in a hot oven before serving.

1 kg/2 lb parsnips
salt and freshly ground black
  pepper
2 tablespoons oil
1 onion, peeled and chopped
450 g/1 lb minced pork
2 tablespoons plain flour

1 chicken stock cube
450 ml/$\frac{3}{4}$ pint water
100 g/4 oz mushrooms, sliced
a little milk
knob of butter
100 g/4 oz matured Cheddar
  cheese, grated

Peel the parsnips, cut them into chunks and cook them in boiling salted water for 20 minutes or until tender.

While the parsnips are cooking, heat the oil in a frying pan and cook the onion until soft but not browned. Stir in the pork and fry, breaking up the meat as it cooks, until lightly browned all over. Stir in the flour, crumble in the stock cube and add the water, then bring to the boil and add the mushrooms. Remove the pan from the heat and stir in seasoning to taste then transfer the meat to a large ovenproof dish.

Drain the cooked parsnips and mash them with a little milk and butter until they are quite smooth. Beat in three-quarters of the cheese, reserving a little to sprinkle over the top of the bake. Cover the meat with the parsnips, spreading them out evenly, and mark the top with a fork. Sprinkle the reserved cheese over and bake in a moderately hot oven (200 C, 400 F, gas 6) for 30 to 40 minutes, or until golden brown on top. Serve at once. **Serves 4**

Stuffed Cabbage Leaves
with Potato Dice

(Illustrated on page 88)

These stuffed cabbage leaves are deliciously different – the filling is not cooked separately so has no tendency to fall apart inside the cabbage, instead it slices meatily and retains its excellent spicy flavour. If you prefer, forget about the potato mixture and serve the cabbage packages on a bed of cooked rice, but I include the potatoes because I think they make the ideal complement.

8 large Savoy cabbage leaves
450 g/1 lb minced pork
1 onion, peeled and very finely chopped
1 large clove garlic, peeled and crushed
4 teaspoons ground cumin
salt and cayenne pepper
1 chicken stock cube
300 ml/½ pint boiling water

2 tablespoons concentrated tomato purée
Potato dice
1 kg/2 lb potatoes
50 g/2 oz butter
1 tablespoon mustard seeds
salt
4 tablespoons water
2 tablespoons chopped fresh coriander leaves or parsley

Trim any very tough stalk ends off the cabbage leaves then cook them briefly in boiling water – allow just 1 minute to soften the leaves so that they will roll up easily. Place the minced pork in a basin then add the onion, garlic, cumin and seasoning. Be careful with the cayenne if you are not used to it: a small pinch should be ample in this dish as it is very hot indeed. Mix all the ingredients thoroughly then roughly divide the mixture into eight portions.

Drain the cabbage leaves and dry them on absorbent kitchen paper. Lay one leaf flat on a board and place a portion of the meat on the middle of the leaf. Fold the stalk end over the filling then fold the sides of the leaf towards the middle. Now roll the leaf neatly and tightly from the stalk end to enclose the filling completely. Continue filling the leaves in this way, placing them neatly in an ovenproof dish with the end of each roll lying underneath.

Dissolve the stock cube in the boiling water then stir in the tomato purée and add just a little salt. Pour this liquid gently over the packages. Cover the dish and bake in a moderately hot oven for 40 to 45 minutes.

While the cabbage leaves are cooking peel and dice the potatoes and rinse them thoroughly. Melt the butter in a large frying pan which has a lid or in a heavy-based saucepan. Add the mustard seeds and stir them round briefly then add the drained potatoes and stir well to coat them in the butter. Add a little salt and fry for a few minutes. Pour in the water and bring to the boil then cover the pan and reduce the heat so the potatoes cook gently. They should be tender in 10 to 15 minutes; do not overcook them or they will become mushy. Increase the heat and boil off any remaining water then sprinkle in the coriander or parsley and transfer the potatoes to a large serving dish or platter, arranging them in a ring round the edge. Lift the cabbage packages carefully into the middle, pouring over a little of the sauce. Serve at once, handing the remaining sauce separately. **Serves 4**

Porky in the Cabbage Patch

This is a good recipe for using up the shredded cabbage which has been taken out of the middle of a Savoy cabbage in order to stuff it (see Stuffed Cabbage with Stilton Cream, page 78). Serve creamed or baked potatoes with this dish.

2 large onions, peeled and
   chopped
4 tablespoons oil
450 g/1 lb minced pork
salt and freshly ground black
   pepper
15 g/$\frac{1}{2}$ oz plain flour
300 ml/$\frac{1}{2}$ pint dry cider or
   chicken stock
100 g/4 oz mushrooms, sliced

1 tablespoon fennel seeds
450–675 g/1–1$\frac{1}{2}$ lb cabbage,
   shredded
Topping
15 g/$\frac{1}{2}$ oz butter
15 g/$\frac{1}{2}$ oz plain flour
300 ml/$\frac{1}{2}$ pint milk
100 g/4 oz Cheddar cheese,
   grated
25 g/1 oz fresh breadcrumbs

Fry one of the onions in half the oil until soft but not browned. Stir in the pork and seasoning to taste and cook, breaking the meat up with a wooden spoon, until lightly browned. Stir in the flour and pour in the cider or stock, still stirring. Bring to the boil, then add the mushrooms and transfer the mixture to an ovenproof dish large enough to leave room for the cabbage. The meat should not come more than about one-third or halfway up the dish.

Wipe the pan you used for cooking the meat then heat the remaining oil in it and fry the second onion, stirring occasionally, until soft but not browned. Add the fennel seeds and cook briefly then add the cabbage. Cook, stirring all the time, until the cabbage is very slightly softened. Add seasoning to taste then lay the cabbage over the meat.

For the topping, melt the butter in a saucepan and stir in the flour. Gradually pour in the milk, stirring all the time, then bring to the boil, still stirring. Add half the grated cheese and seasoning to taste, then pour this sauce over the cabbage to coat the top completely.

Mix the remaining cheese with the breadcrumbs and sprinkle over the sauce. Bake in a moderately hot oven (200 C, 400 F, gas 6) for 30 minutes, or until the top of the dish is golden brown and crisp. Serve at once. **Serves 4**

Peppered Pork Loaf

To many people, meatloaf suggests beef mixed with plenty of breadcrumbs to make it go as far as possible, baked to death, possibly with a row of hard-boiled eggs down the middle. However, meatloaf can be both varied and marvellous – here is just one recipe for pork and sweet pepper mixture. Good hot or equally tasty cold, this versatile dish can be served with a creamy Mushroom Sauce (see page 162) or with Garlic Mayonnaise (see page 170) and salad.

450 g/1 lb minced pork
1 large red pepper
1 large green pepper
1 onion, peeled and finely
  chopped

50 g/2 oz fresh breadcrumbs
100 g/4 oz Philadelphia cheese
salt and freshly ground black
  pepper
1 egg, beaten

Put the pork in a large bowl. Cut the peppers in half, remove stalks, pith and seeds, chop the flesh and add to the meat. Stir in the remaining ingredients, mixing thoroughly until all is well combined.

Line the base of a 1-kg/2-lb loaf tin with a piece of greaseproof paper. Grease the base and sides of the tin thoroughly then put the meat in the tin. Smooth the top and bake the meat loaf in a moderately hot oven (200 C, 400 F, gas 6) for 1 hour.

To serve, turn the loaf out on to a dish (to catch the juices), then remove the paper and slice the meat. Alternatively allow the meatloaf to cool in the tin and turn it out when cold. **Serves 4 to 6**

Peppered Pork Loaf with Pineapple
If you like, add a layer of canned pineapple to the above meatloaf. Put half the meat mixture in the lined and greased tin, then top with drained canned pineapple (fruit canned in natural juice is best for this). Put the remaining meat mixture in the tin, press down well and continue as above.

Chilli Stuffed Peppers

These baked peppers have a pork filling which is seasoned with a little chilli powder and cumin. If you like you can substitute minced beef for the pork, or even minced lamb. Serve cooked rice with the peppers.

4 red or green peppers
1 onion, peeled and chopped
450 g/1 lb minced pork
2 teaspoons chilli powder
2 teaspoons ground cumin
4 sticks of celery, finely
    chopped
salt and freshly ground black
    pepper

1 beef stock cube
300 ml/½ pint boiling water
1 (397-g/14-oz) can chopped
    tomatoes
bay leaf
1 clove garlic, crushed
100 g/4 oz cream cheese

Cut the tops off the peppers to form neat lids and remove any seeds and pith from the insides. Wash them thoroughly. If necessary, trim just a sliver of pepper from the bases to make the peppers stand neatly but take care not to cut a hole in them.

For the filling, mix the onion into the pork, add the chilli powder, cumin and celery and mix them thoroughly, stirring in seasoning to taste. Make sure the meat is well broken up and combined with the other ingredients. Divide the mixture between the peppers, pressing it down into the shells, then stand the stuffed peppers in an ovenproof dish.

Dissolve the stock cube in the boiling water, then stir in the tomatoes and bay leaf with a little seasoning. Pour this sauce round the peppers, then put their lids on and cover with cooking foil. Bake in a moderately hot oven (200 C, 400 F, gas 6) for 1 hour.

Beat the garlic into the cream cheese. Divide the mixture into four equal portions then shape each into a small round cake about the size of the top of the peppers. Chill thoroughly.

To serve, lift the lids off the peppers (do this carefully with a round-bladed knife), then top each with a portion of the garlic-flavoured cheese. Replace the lids and serve at once. **Serves 4**

PASTRY DISHES, PIZZAS AND PANCAKES

A mixed bag of old favourites and some interesting new recipes make this chapter a good one to thumb through – it provides ideas for most occasions. For family meals, elegant buffets and carefree summer picnics, the pies will certainly recommend themselves; but such delicacies as mince-filled pancakes and pizzas offer a slightly unusual repertoire for more adventurous menu planning.

Turkey Jalousie

A jalousie consists of two layers of puff pastry with a sweet or savoury filling. The top of the pastry is cut into slats. Layered with cranberry sauce, ham and almonds, this turkey-filled jalousie is ideal hot for dinner parties or cold for more informal buffets. Serve White Wine Sauce (page 164) with the dish if you are eating it hot.

1 (368-g/13-oz) packet frozen puff pastry, thawed
4 tablespoons cranberry sauce
4 slices cooked ham
450 g/1 lb minced turkey
salt and freshly ground black pepper
2 tablespoons chopped parsley
1 small onion, peeled and grated
50 g/2 oz fresh breadcrumbs
150 ml/$\frac{1}{4}$ pint soured cream
50 g/2 oz flaked almonds
1 egg, beaten

Cut the pastry in half. On a lightly floured surface, roll out one piece to an oblong shape 12 × 30 cm/5 × 12 in. Lift it on to a baking tray and spread the cranberry sauce over the middle, leaving a 2.5-cm/1-in border all round the edge. Lay the ham, overlapping the slices generously, or folding them in half, on top of the cranberry sauce.

Mix the turkey with the seasoning to taste, parsley, onion and breadcrumbs. Stir in the soured cream then spoon this mixture over the ham, keeping the border of the pastry clear. Sprinkle the flaked almonds over the mixture.

Roll the second portion of the pastry into an oblong slightly larger than the first – this time make it 18 × 35.5 cm/7 × 14 in – and lightly fold it in half down its length. Without pressing the pastry together too firmly, cut slits from within 2.5 cm/1 in of the long edge of the pastry right through the fold, leaving a border at both ends of the pastry. The slits should be about 2.5 cm/1 in wide. Brush the edge of the pastry with a little of the beaten egg then carefully unfold this slatted lid and place it on top of the turkey mixture, pressing the edges together firmly to seal in the filling at the sides.

Brush the top of the pastry all over with beaten egg then bake the jalousie in a moderately hot oven (200 C, 400 F, gas 6) for 45 to 50 minutes, or until the pastry is golden and puffed and the filling is cooked through.

To serve the jalousie, carefully use two large fish slices to lift it off the baking tray and on to a warmed serving platter. **Serves 4 to 6**

Mince and Kidney Pie

175 g/6 oz lambs' kidneys
2 tablespoons oil
1 large onion, peeled and
 chopped
450 g/1 lb minced beef
2 tablespoons plain flour
salt and freshly ground black
 pepper

1 beef stock cube
1 tablespoon concentrated
 tomato purée
600 ml/1 pint water
100 g/4 oz mushrooms, sliced
1 (368-g/13-oz) packet frozen
 puff pastry, thawed
beaten egg or milk to glaze

Cut the kidneys in half then remove their cores (it's easiest to snip them out with a pair of kitchen scissors) and chop them into small pieces. Heat the oil in a large frying pan and fry the onion until soft but not browned.

Stir in the kidney and minced beef and continue cooking over a fairly high heat until the meat is lightly browned. Stir continuously as the beef cooks to break it up evenly and ensure even cooking. Stir in the flour and seasoning to taste, crumble in the stock cube and add the tomato purée. Gradually pour in the water then bring to the boil, stirring frequently. Add the mushrooms and remove pan from heat.

Have ready a 1.15-litre/2-pint pie dish. On a lightly floured surface roll out the pastry until it is about 5 cm/2 in larger than the top of the dish. Cut a 2.5-cm/1-in strip of pastry off the edge, dampen it on one side and press it on to the rim of the dish. Spoon the meat filling into the dish, dampen the pastry edge and lift the lid on top. Press the edges together well to seal in the filling. Trim off and reserve any excess pastry, then knock up the edges to seal them together. To do this, gently tap the edge of the pastry with the blunt edge of a knife blade, holding the pastry in place with the index finger of your left hand. Pinch the edge of the pastry into scallop shapes and roll out the trimmings to make leaves for the top of the pie. Cut a small hole in the middle of the pie to allow steam to escape. Brush the pie with beaten egg or milk, then bake it in a hot oven (220 C, 425 F, gas 7) for 40 to 45 minutes, or until well risen and browned. Serve immediately. **Serves 4**

Herb-crusted Beef Pie

This is a good, homely beef pie, with small sausages stirred into the filling and some lively herbs used to make the pastry more interesting.

2 tablespoons oil
225 g/8 oz cocktail pork
  sausages
1 large onion, peeled and
  chopped
450 g/1 lb minced beef
salt and freshly ground black
  pepper
2 tablespoons plain flour
450 ml/¾ pint brown ale
1 beef stock cube
100 g/4 oz button mushrooms,
  sliced

Herb pastry
225 g/8 oz plain flour
pinch of salt
2 tablespoons chopped parsley
1 teaspoon thyme
1 teaspoon marjoram
½ teaspoon rubbed sage
100 g/4 oz margarine or half and
  half lard and margarine
about 4 tablespoons cold water

Prepare the filling first. Heat the oil in a large frying pan or heavy-based saucepan and cook the sausages until golden all over. Remove them from the pan and drain them on absorbent kitchen paper. Add the onion to the fat remaining in the pan and cook until soft but not browned. Stir in the meat, breaking it up as it cooks, then add the seasoning and flour. Stir well for a minute, then slowly pour in the ale and crumble in the stock cube. Bring to the boil, reduce the heat and simmer for 20 minutes uncovered so that some of the excess liquid evaporates. Lastly, add the mushrooms and taste the filling for seasoning. Allow it to cool – it does not have to be cold but if too hot it will melt the pastry lid. Stir in the sausages just before using the filling.

To make the pastry sift the flour into a bowl and add a pinch of salt. Stir in the herbs, add the fat cut into small pieces and rub the fat into the flour until the mixture resembles fine breadcrumbs. Stir in the water and clump the mixture together lightly to make a short dough. Have ready a 1.15-litre/2-pint pie dish. Turn the pastry on to a floured work surface and roll it out about 5 cm/2 in larger than the dish. Cut a strip from the edge, dampen it on the underside and press it on to the rim of the dish. Put the filling in the dish, dampen the pastry rim then put the lid on top. Trim the pastry and knock up the edge to seal in the filling. Use the trimmings to make leaves to decorate the top of the pie. Secure these with a little beaten egg, glaze the pie with a more beaten egg and bake it in a moderately hot oven (200 C, 400 F, gas 6) for about 45 to 50 minutes, or until golden brown. Serve at once. **Serves 4**

Baked Suet Pudding

Suet-crust pastry is delicious baked in the oven – it rises and becomes light with a golden crust. This is a heart-warming dish to serve for cold winter days. Onion Gravy (see page 43) would go very well with the pudding.

225 g/8 oz minced pork
225 g/8 oz minced beef
  (alternatively use all beef)
1 large onion, peeled and
  chopped
100 g/4 oz button mushrooms,
  sliced
salt and freshly ground black
  pepper

1 beef stock cube
100 ml/4 fl oz boiling water
bay leaf
Pastry
225 g/8 oz self-raising flour
½ teaspoon salt
100 g/4 oz shredded suet
150 ml/¼ pint cold water

Mix the minced meats in a bowl, add the onion and mushrooms and a little seasoning. Dissolve the stock cube in the boiling water, then pour it into the mince mixture and stir well. Add the bay leaf.

To make the pastry, sift the flour into a bowl with the salt. Stir in the suet then pour in the water and mix to make a soft dough. Turn the dough out on to a lightly floured surface and knead lightly. Grease a 1.15-litre/2-pint ovenproof pudding basin (for example, Pyrex). Cut off and reserve one-third of the pastry for the lid, and lightly roll out the rest into a circle large enough to line the basin. Ease it in, pressing it against the sides and leaving enough at the rim to fold over the lid. Put the meat mixture into the basin then roll out the remaining pastry into a circle large enough to just cover the top. Lift it over the pudding, dampen the edge and fold the pastry rim down over the lid, pressing it on firmly to seal in the filling.

Stand the basin on a baking tray and cook in a moderately hot oven (200 C, 400 F, gas 6) for 1 hour. Invert the basin on to a warmed serving dish and serve at once. **Serves 4**

Peppered Beef Pizza

This is a good and meaty main dish – well seasoned minced beef is spread thickly over a bread crust. The whole pizza is then topped with mushrooms, olives, anchovies and cheese. A salad would go very well – try the Avocado and Orange Salad on page 173 for example.

½ (275-g/10-oz) packet bread
  mix
Topping
450 g/1 lb minced beef
1 large clove garlic, peeled and
  crushed
1 small onion, peeled and grated
2 tablespoons concentrated
  tomato purée
1 teaspoon paprika

salt and freshly ground black
  pepper
1 red pepper
1 green pepper
225 g/8 oz mozzarella cheese
1 (50-g/2-oz) can anchovies
100 g/4 oz button mushrooms,
  sliced
a few black olives

First make up the bread mix according to the packet instructions, but using half the quantity of water. Roll it out into a 25-cm/10-in circle and place this on a greased baking tray. Fold the edge back to form a neat rim then leave the dough, covered with a piece of cling film, in a warm place while you prepare the topping.

Mix the beef with the garlic, onion and tomato purée then stir in the paprika and seasoning to taste. Cut the tops off the peppers, remove all the seeds and pith from inside and cut into fine rings. Slice the cheese thinly. Drain the oil from the anchovies and reserve it for brushing the top of the pizza, then cut the fillets in half lengthways.

Uncover the pizza base and put the mince mixture on top, spreading it evenly and patting it into shape like a big hamburger. Arrange the sliced mushrooms on top of the meat, then add the pepper rings. Cover with the cheese and arrange the anchovies and olives in a lattice pattern on top. Sprinkle the reserved anchovy oil over the pizza and bake it in a hot oven (220 C, 425 F, gas 7) for 40 to 45 minutes, until the meat and topping are golden and the base is cooked through.

Serve the pizza piping hot, cut into large wedges. **Serves 4 to 6**

Chilli Calzone

This recipe is an odd mixture of ideas. A calzone is an Italian creation, a sort of pizza which is folded in half to enclose the cheese filling in a light and crisp bread crust. Here the bread crust is folded around a chilli-spiced beef mixture which is topped with Italian cheese. The result is a multi-national concoction which actually tastes very good!

½ (560-g/20-oz) packet bread
   mix
Filling
2 tablespoons olive oil
2 cloves garlic, peeled and
   crushed
1 large onion, peeled and
   chopped
450 g/1 lb minced beef
2 tablespoons ground coriander

1 tablespoon chilli powder
salt and freshly ground black
   pepper
1 (326-g/11.5-oz) can sweet
   corn, drained
350 g/12 oz mozzarella cheese,
   sliced
1 teaspoon marjoram
½ teaspoon chopped dried
   thyme

Make up the bread mix according to the recipe instructions, but using half the quantity of water. Roll out the dough to make a large circle – about 35.5 cm/14 in. in diameter. Grease a baking tray or a roasting tin and lay the dough on top – it will eventually be folded in half like a pasty, so don't worry if it seems far too large for the container at this stage.

For the filling, heat the oil in a large frying pan and fry the garlic, then the onion, until soft but not browned. Stir in the beef and cook briefly, then mix in the coriander and chilli powder. Stir well then add seasoning to taste and the sweet corn; remove the pan from the heat and spread the mixture over half the rolled-out dough. Top with the cheese, then sprinkle the herbs over. Brush the edges of the dough with a little water and fold the uncovered side over to enclose the filling completely in a half-moon shaped pasty. Pinch the edges well together to seal in the filling then cut off any excess.

Bake the calzone in a hot oven (220 C, 425 F, gas 7) for about 40 minutes or until browned and cooked through. Serve cut into wedges.
Serves 4 to 6

Samosas

*These crisp and light, spicy pasties are an Indian snack food. The filling in
this recipe is not chilli-hot so, if you like, add about ½ teaspoon chilli powder
to the meat.*

100 g/4 oz plain flour
pinch of salt
50 ml/2 fl oz water
1 tablespoon oil
Filling
1 onion, peeled and finely
  chopped
1 clove garlic, peeled and
  crushed
2 tablespoons oil

1 teaspoon mustard seeds
2 green cardamoms
1 tablespoon ground cumin
1 tablespoon ground coriander
225 g/8 oz minced beef
salt and freshly ground black
  pepper
4 tablespoons water
oil for deep frying

To make the dough, sift the flour into a bowl and add the salt. Make a
well in the middle, then pour in the water and add the oil. Gradually
stir the flour into the liquid to make a firm dough then knead the
ingredients together, continuing until the dough becomes smooth and
quite elastic. Wrap it in cling film and set it aside while you prepare the
filling.

Fry the onion and garlic in the oil until the onion is soft but not
browned. Add the spices and cook for 2 to 3 minutes, stirring
continuously, then add the meat and cook, breaking it up with a
wooden spoon, until lightly fried. Add plenty of seasoning and the
water then bring to the boil and simmer until the water has evaporated.
Set aside to cool.

To fill and shape the samosas, cut the dough into eight equal portions
and roll each piece in turn into a long narrow strip measuring about 23
× 8.5 cm/9 × 3½ in. Trim one short end so that it is straight, then place
a little filling about 2.5 cm/1 in away from the edge. Fold one corner
across the filling to cover it and form a triangular shape. Fold the filling
and its cover over again in the opposite direction. Continue folding the
triangular pasty over and over, down the length of the pastry strip,
until the whole strip is used. When you have only a short piece of
dough left, trim the end straight, brush it with a little water then fold it
neatly over the pasty and press it down well to seal in the filling.

Heat the oil to 180 C/350 F, or until a cube of bread browns in 30
seconds, then fry the samosas a few at a time until they are golden,
turning them over during cooking. Drain on absorbent kitchen paper
and serve hot, warm or cold. **Makes 8**

Opposite page *Top: Empanada (page 114); Below: Spicy Cornbread
Pizza (page 129)* **Overleaf** *Clockwise from the top: Pork and Apple
Plait (page 124), Lamb Pasties (page 119) and Highland Pies (page
116)*

Savoury Pancake Rolls

Baked pancakes filled with a meaty mixture and topped with a full-flavoured cheese sauce are very tasty indeed. The pancakes and filling can be made and frozen with the sauce poured over. They can then be stored for about 6 months and baked just before eating.

Pancake batter
100 g/4 oz plain flour
pinch of salt
2 eggs, beaten
300 ml/½ pint milk
oil or butter for cooking
Filling
50 g/2 oz butter
1 large onion, peeled and
  chopped
1 clove garlic, peeled and
  crushed
450 g/1 lb minced beef

1 tablespoon plain flour
salt and freshly ground black
  pepper
1 (397-g/14-oz) can chopped
  tomatoes
300 ml/½ pint red wine
2 teaspoons dried mixed herbs
1 quantity Cheese Sauce (page
  162)
100 g/4 oz button mushrooms,
  roughly chopped
50 g/2 oz flaked almonds

To make the pancake batter, sift the flour and salt into a bowl and make a well in the middle. Pour the eggs into the well and add the milk little by little, beating all the time, and gradually mixing in the flour to make a smooth batter. When you are satisfied that there are no lumps set the batter aside and prepare the pancake filling.

Melt the butter in a heavy-based saucepan and cook the onion until soft but not browned. Stir in the garlic and meat and fry until the beef is evenly browned, breaking it up with a wooden spoon as it cooks. Add the flour and seasoning to taste, pour in the tomatoes and the wine then stir in the herbs and bring to the boil. Reduce the heat and simmer gently, uncovered, while you cook the pancakes.

Cook thin pancakes in a large, lightly oiled or buttered pan until they are browned on both sides. If you are unfamiliar with the technique of cooking pancakes, follow the instructions for Spinach Pancake and Pork Layer (see page 130). Stack the pancakes with pieces of absorbent kitchen paper between each one.

When they are all cooked, prepare the cheese sauce according to the recipe instructions. Stir the mushrooms into the mince. Place a little of the meat in each of the pancakes, roll up and transfer to an ovenproof dish. Pour the sauce over the top and sprinkle with the almonds. Bake in a moderately hot oven (200 C, 400 F, gas 6) for 30 minutes, until bubbling and golden. Serve immediately. **Serves 4**

Top: Spinach Pancake and Pork Layer (page 130); Below: Mexicali Pancakes (page 118)

Cornish Pasties

Home-made Cornish pasties have nothing at all to do with the many poor imitations which can be bought pre-packed or frozen, but since the days when I learnt to make pastry at school these simple pasties have all but disappeared. When I tested this recipe I realised how easy it would be to make a couple of dozen at a time and freeze them uncooked ready for baking when needed. If you do this, open-freeze the pasties on a baking tray before packing them in an airtight bag; they will keep for up to 6 months.

Shortcrust pastry
450 g/1 lb plain flour
salt and freshly ground black
    pepper
generous 225 g/8 oz margarine or
    half and half lard and
    margarine
about 8 tablespoons cold water
Filling
450 g/1 lb minced beef
450 g/1 lb potatoes, peeled and
    finely diced

225 g/8 oz carrots, finely diced
1 small onion, peeled and finely
    chopped
1 teaspoon chopped dried
    thyme
2 teaspoons chopped parsley
generous dash of Worcestershire
    sauce
4 tablespoons beef stock or
    water
beaten egg to glaze

To make the pastry sift the flour into a bowl and add a pinch of salt. Cut the fat into small pieces and add to the flour, then rub in with your fingertips until the mixture resembles fine breadcrumbs. Gradually add the water, stirring with a round-bladed knife until the mixture starts to clump together. Use your hand to lightly knead the pastry together into a ball of dough. Divide the pastry into six equal portions.

For the filling, mix the ingredients together in a basin, adding plenty of seasoning. Make sure the liquid is well mixed into the meat and that all the ingredients are evenly distributed.

On a lightly floured surface roll out each piece of the pastry in turn to make a 20-cm/8-in circle. Keep it as neat as possible, but there is no need to trim any off at this stage. Place a sixth of the filling in the middle of each piece then brush all round the edge with a little of the beaten egg and carefully fold the pastry up over the filling to join the opposite sides in the middle. Press the edges together well to seal in the filling thoroughly. Use a pair of kitchen scissors to trim off just the very edge of the pastry, then flute the join between your thumb and forefinger.

Place the pasties on a greased baking tray, brush with a little beaten egg and bake in a moderately hot oven (200 C, 400 F, gas 6), for 45 minutes. The pasties are best served about 30 minutes after they have been removed from the oven, when they are just the right temperature for eating. **Makes 6**

Double Crust Veal and Asparagus Pie

Serve this delicious but quite substantial pie hot with a White Wine Sauce (see page 164), buttered new potatoes and a Green Salad (see page 172).

Rich shortcrust pastry
350 g/12 oz plain flour
salt and freshly ground black
   pepper
225 g/8 oz butter or margarine
about 6 tablespoons cold water
Filling
675 g/1½ lb minced veal
1 large onion, peeled and finely
   chopped

grated rind of 1 lemon
100 g/4 oz button mushrooms,
   chopped
1 tablespoon chopped fresh
   thyme
150 ml/¼ pint dry white wine
1 (227-g/8-oz) packet frozen
   asparagus, thawed and
   drained
beaten egg to glaze

To make the pastry, sift the flour into a bowl and add a pinch of salt. Cut the butter or margarine into small pieces and add to the flour, rubbing in with your fingers until the mixture resembles fine breadcrumbs. Sprinkle in the water, mixing all the time with a round-bladed knife, and when the pastry begins to clump together, knead it lightly.

Mix the veal with the onion, lemon rind, mushrooms and thyme. Add a generous sprinkling of seasoning and stir in the wine. Cook the asparagus following the packet instructions then drain thoroughly.

Have ready a 25-cm/10-in deep pie plate. Cut off about two-thirds of the pastry and roll it out on a lightly floured surface into a circle large enough to line the plate. Lift the pastry over the rolling pin and put it on the plate, pressing it down well, and making sure there is plenty of pastry on the rim. Spread about half of the meat mixture in the lined pie plate, then arrange the spears of asparagus on top. Cover the asparagus with the remaining meat, piling it up in the middle.

Roll out the remaining pastry into a circle to cover the pie, remembering to make it large enough to cover all the filling and leave room to seal the edges. Brush the rim of the pastry base with a little water, lift the pastry lid on to it, press the edges together well and trim off the excess. Reserve this for making leaves to decorate the pie. Knock up the pastry edge with the back of a knife to seal the edge thoroughly, flute the pastry edge between your thumb and forefinger then brush the pie all over with beaten egg. Roll out the trimmings and cut out leaves, secure these on the pie with egg and then glaze.

Bake the pie in a moderate oven (180 C, 350 F, gas 4) for 1 hour or until golden brown and cooked through. **Serves 4 to 6**

Veal and Ham Pie

(Illustrated on front cover)

Classic traditional dishes such as this one survive the test of years because they are delicious and worth the effort involved. There is no really quick way of making a superb pie of this type, though instead of hot-water crust pastry I used shortcrust to line the loaf tin and was quite pleased with the result. Serve the pie cold, cut into fairly thick slices, with salads and baked potatoes. The pie is perfect for taking on picnics, presents itself well on a cold buffet table and turns a lunch-box meal into something rather special.

Shortcrust pastry
350 g/12 oz plain flour
salt and freshly ground black
   pepper
175 g/6 oz margarine or half and
   half lard and margarine
about 6–8 tablespoons cold
   water
Filling
575–675 g/1¼–1½ lb gammon

1 kg/2 lb minced veal
2 teaspoons ground mace
1 large onion, peeled and finely
   chopped
generous sprinkling freshly
   grated nutmeg
4 tablespoons chopped parsley
6 tablespoons water
beaten egg to glaze

Soak the gammon overnight or for several hours in enough cold water to cover it.

To make the pastry, sift the flour into a bowl and add a pinch of salt. Cut the fat into small pieces, add to the flour and rub in with your fingertips until the mixture resembles fine breadcrumbs. Sprinkle in the cold water, stirring the pastry with a round-bladed knife, until the mixture just begins to clump together. Lightly knead the dough together. Once the pastry is made, it can be wrapped in cling film and set aside until the filling is prepared. There is no need to chill it unless the room is very warm.

Drain the soaked gammon and trim off the rind and all the fat (the trimmed weight should be about 450 g/1 lb or very slightly less). Chop the meat and place it in a bowl with the veal. Add the remaining filling ingredients and seasoning, but be careful not to overseason in case the gammon is salty.

Grease a 1-kg/2-lb loaf tin. Roll out three-quarters of the pastry into an oblong shape large enough to line the loaf tin. Keep checking the size by placing the tin in the middle of the pastry. Carefully lift the pastry into the tin, making the corners as neat as possible. You will have to overlap the pastry at the corners to make it fit well. Allow enough pastry at the top of the tin to form a high edge.

Put the meat filling in the pastry case, piling it up well in the middle. The filling will shrink during cooking so it should form quite a high mound down the middle of the tin at this stage. Roll out the remaining pastry to form a lid, remembering to make it large enough to cover the piled-up meat and tuck in well at the sides. Brush the edge of the pastry case with a little water, then lift on the lid, pressing it neatly around the meat and down at the sides. Press the pastry edges together well and trim off any excess. Pinch the edge between your fingers to make a decorative border, then make a small hole in the middle of the pie for the steam to escape. Roll out the pastry trimmings and cut out leaves or other shapes to decorate the middle of the pie. Make the decorations fairly lavish, and secure them to the pie with a little of the beaten egg. Brush the top of the pie with beaten egg, then stand the tin on a Swiss roll tin (or similar) and bake in a moderate oven (180 C, 350 F, gas 5) for $1\frac{1}{2}$ hours. Check during cooking and brush a little extra egg on top to give a good, even glaze.

Allow the pie to cool completely in the tin, then carefully run a knife along the sides to loosen the pastry. Invert the pie into your hand (best to do this over a board or something just in case you do let it slip) and remove the tin. If the base of the pie is stuck in the tin, then hold it over a gas flame or electric ring for about half a minute to warm the juices and loosen the base. Stand the pie on a serving dish and add a garnish of salad ingredients, or cut it into slices and arrange them on a dish.
Serves 8

Note. If your loaf tin is at all likely to stick, then it's a good idea to line the base with greaseproof paper before putting the pastry in.

Empanada

(Illustrated on page 105)

*A Spanish empanada can be either a pie or several individual pasties, with
a crust which may be yeast based and a filling which varies according to the
region and the availability of ingredients. Here is a recipe which does not
attempt absolute authenticity but offers a colourful combination of lively
ingredients in an unsophisticated wrapping. You can, if you like, substitute
a packet of bread mix quite successfully for the yeast dough, in which case
follow the recipe instructions for making up the mixture.*

Dough
150 ml/¼ pint lukewarm water
1 teaspoon sugar
3 teaspoons dried yeast
225 g/8 oz strong plain flour
50 g/2 oz butter
½ teaspoon salt
Filling
1 large green pepper
1 green chilli
2 tablespoons olive oil
2 cloves garlic, peeled and
  crushed

1 Spanish onion, peeled and
  chopped
175 g/6 oz chorizos (spicy
  Spanish sausage, available
  from delicatessens)
450 g/1 lb minced beef
salt and freshly ground black
  pepper
50 g/2 oz raisins
1 (397-g/14-oz) can chopped
  tomatoes
4 hard-boiled eggs

Pour the water into a basin and stir in the sugar, then sprinkle in the
yeast and set the liquid aside in a warm place for about 30 minutes until
frothy.

Sift the flour into a bowl and add the butter, cut into small pieces.
Mix in the salt then rub the fat into the flour until the mixture
resembles fine breadcrumbs. Give the yeast liquid a good stir, then add
it to the flour and mix it in to make a smooth dough. Turn out on to a
lightly floured surface and knead thoroughly for about 10 minutes or
until smooth and elastic. Put the dough in a lightly oiled bowl, cover
with cling film or a damp tea-towel and leave in a warm place until
doubled in size.

Meanwhile, prepare the filling. Cut the pepper in half, remove all the
seeds and pith from inside and chop the flesh. Cut the stalk end off the
chilli, split the shell and wash out all the seeds from inside. Finely chop
the chilli. (Be careful if you are unused to handling chillies: do not rub
your eyes as the juices will burn them.) Heat the oil in a large frying pan
or saucepan and cook the pepper, chilli, garlic and onion until the
onion is soft but not browned, stirring well. Cut the chorizos into fine
slices and add to the pan. Increase the heat slightly and fry, stirring
frequently, for a few minutes. Add the beef and cook, breaking up the
meat, until lightly browned. Stir in seasoning to taste, the raisins and
the tomatoes. Bring to the boil then remove the pan from the heat.

Roughly chop the eggs and add them to the mixture.

Have ready an ovenproof dish measuring about 25–30 cm/10–12 in. in diameter. A quiche dish or paella pan would be suitable, or a similar shallow tin. Briefly knead the risen dough then cut about two-thirds off and roll it out to line the dish, making sure there is plenty of extra dough round the edge. Lay the dough in the dish, there is no need to be too fussy about pressing it into the corners. Pile the prepared filling on top. Roll out the remaining dough to just cover the filling, place it on top then brush the top with a little water and fold over the edges of the dough lining to seal in the filling completely. Bake in a moderately hot oven (200 C, 400 F, gas 6) for 30 to 35 minutes. Cut the pie into wedges to serve. **Serves 6 to 8**

Veal and Apple Pasties with Walnuts

Serve these pasties either hot or cold, with baked potatoes and salads or a moist vegetable dish such as ratatouille (see Ratatouille Beef Ring, page 132).

1 quantity shortcrust pastry (see
   Veal and Ham Pie, page 112)
beaten egg to glaze
Filling
450 g/1 lb minced veal
1 large cooking apple, peeled,
   cored and diced
50 g/2 oz chopped walnuts
1 small onion, peeled and finely
   chopped

2 tablespoons chopped mixed
   fresh herbs; for example
   thyme, parsley, sage,
   marjoram, rosemary
salt and freshly ground black
   pepper
50 g/2 oz raisins

Make the pastry according to the recipe instructions and divide it into six equal portions. Mix all the filling ingredients together, making sure the meat is well seasoned.

Roll out each portion of pastry in turn into a 20-cm/8-in circle, put a sixth of the filling in the middle and dampen the edge. Fold opposite sides of the pastry up to meet over the filling and pinch the edges together, making sure they are well sealed. Trim off excess pastry and flute the seams, then place the pasties on a baking tray and brush with a little beaten egg.

Bake the pasties in a moderately hot oven (200 C, 400 F, gas 6) for 50–60 minutes. Serve hot, or leave on a wire rack to cool. **Makes 6**

Highland Pies

(Illustrated on pages 106/107)

Scotch mutton pies are a traditional recipe from the north. Filled with meat and spices, they have an outer shell of hot-water crust pastry.

450 g/1 lb minced lamb
1 onion, peeled and finely
    chopped
$\frac{1}{2}$ teaspoon ground mace
generous sprinkling of freshly
    grated nutmeg
salt and freshly ground black
    pepper
1 small potato, peeled and finely
    diced

4 tablespoons water
2 tablespoons chopped parsley
Hot-water crust pastry
350 g/12 oz plain flour
$\frac{1}{2}$ teaspoon salt
100 g/4 oz margarine
4 tablespoons water
4 tablespoons milk
beaten egg to glaze

Mix the lamb with all the other filling ingredients, making sure the mixture is thoroughly combined and well seasoned.

Prepare six jam jars to mould the pies, as follows. Upturn them and cover their bases with foil, moulding it tightly on to each jar, then brush the foil lightly with oil.

To make the pastry, sift the flour and salt into a bowl. Put the margarine, water and milk into a saucepan and heat gently until the fat melts then bring rapidly to the boil. Pour the liquid over the flour, mixing all the time, then knead the dough together with your hand, taking great care as it will be very hot to touch. Divide the dough into six equal portions. Keep five of these hot in a bowl over a saucepan of hot water, covered with a piece of cling film.

Lightly knead one portion of dough until smooth, then cut off a third and put it with the rest in the bowl – this is for the lid. Roll out the piece of dough to give a 14-cm/5$\frac{1}{2}$-in round and mould it on to one of the jam jars to make a neat case. Tie a double band of greaseproof paper round the pastry and leave in a cool place until set. Repeat this process with the other five portions.

When the pastry cases have cooled and set, ease them off the jars, place them on a greased baking tray, and fill them with the meat mixture. Roll out the reserved pieces of pastry to make lids and press these in place, sealing the edges with a little beaten egg. Make a small round hole in the middle of each pie to let the air escape and trim the edges of any excess pastry, leaving them quite plain. Brush with beaten egg, leaving the greaseproof paper bands in place, bake in a moderately hot oven (200 C, 400 F, gas 6) for 20 minutes, then carefully remove the greaseproof paper, brush the outside of the pies with beaten egg and cook for a further 15 to 20 minutes or until the pies are browned.

Remove the pies from the trays and serve them hot with Onion Gravy (see page 43) or allow them to cool on a wire rack. **Makes 6**

Puff-crust Lamb Rolls

This is an excellent dinner-party recipe, and it's not too expensive. Serve simple vegetables – like new potatoes, broccoli or French beans, all with a little butter, and chopped mint on the potatoes – and Red Wine Sauce (see page 164) with the rolls. The rolls can be made in advance, wrapped in pastry and decorated, then frozen ready for cooking before dinner. Cook the rolls from frozen but reduce the oven temperature once the pastry has puffed and allow a few minutes extra cooking time to make sure the meat is thoroughly cooked in the middle.

450 g/1 lb minced lamb
50 g/2 oz dried apricots (use the
    type which do not require
    pre-soaking)
1 small onion, peeled and very
    finely chopped
2 tablespoons chopped fresh
    tarragon

salt and freshly ground black
    pepper
1 (397-g/13-oz) packet frozen
    puff pastry, thawed
1 egg, beaten
Garnish
orange slices
sprigs of watercress

Mix the lamb with the apricots, onion, tarragon and seasoning to taste. Make sure the ingredients are all thoroughly and evenly combined then divide the mixture into four equal portions and shape these into rolls measuring about 10 cm/4 in long.

Divide the pastry into four equal portions and roll out each piece in turn on a lightly floured surface to an oblong measuring 20 × 15 cm/8 × 6 in. Use a 5-cm/2-in fluted pastry cutter to cut out two circles from one end of each piece, then trim the end straight again. Trim the other edges, reserving all the trimmings for decoration. Place a lamb roll on each piece of pastry, brush the edges with a little beaten egg and fold the pastry over the meat to enclose it completely. Trim any excess pastry from the ends but retain enough to fold down over the edge of the roll. Brush the circles of pastry with beaten egg and press one on to each end of each roll. Re-roll the trimmings, cut out leaves to decorate the tops of the rolls, secure them with a little egg then place them on a baking tray and brush with more beaten egg.

Bake in a hot oven (220 C, 425 F, gas 7) for 40 minutes. The pastry should be well puffed and browned and the meat cooked through. Transfer the rolls to the serving plate or on to individual plates and add a garnish of orange slices and watercress. Serve at once. **Serves 4**

Mexicali Pancakes

(Illustrated on page 108 and front cover)

Golden corn pancakes filled with spicy beef and pork and topped with soured cream and avocados makes a tempting meal for any occasion. Spinach and Bacon Salad (see page 173) is an ideal accompaniment to these pancakes.

Pancake batter
75 g/3 oz cornmeal
25 g/1 oz plain flour
salt and freshly ground black
    pepper
2 eggs
300–450 ml/$\frac{1}{2}$–$\frac{3}{4}$ pint milk
oil or butter for cooking
Filling
1 green pepper
1 large onion, peeled and finely
    chopped
1 clove garlic, peeled and
    crushed
2 tablespoons peanut oil

225 g/8 oz minced beef
225 g/8 oz minced pork
150 ml/$\frac{1}{4}$ pint boiling water
1 beef stock cube
1 (397-g/14-oz) can chopped
    tomatoes
1 teaspoon chilli powder
Topping
2 large ripe avocado pears
juice of $\frac{1}{2}$ lemon
1 clove garlic, peeled and
    crushed
150 ml/$\frac{1}{4}$ pint double cream
2 tablespoons chopped fresh
    coriander leaves

To make the pancakes, put the cornmeal in a bowl and add the flour, then sprinkle in plenty of seasoning. Make a well in the middle of the dry ingredients, break the eggs into it and beat them well, gradually working in the dry ingredients, and at the same time pouring in 300 ml/$\frac{1}{2}$ pint of the milk a little at a time. Beat until the batter is quite smooth, then set it aside while you prepare the filling. (The batter should be left to stand for about 30 minutes, longer if possible.)

Cut the pepper in half, slice off the stalk ends, remove all the pith and seeds from inside and slice the flesh into strips and then into fine dice. Put the pepper, onion and garlic into a large frying pan, add the oil, heat slowly and fry until the onion and pepper are thoroughly softened. Add both types of mince and cook over a moderate heat, breaking the meat up as it cooks, until lightly browned. Pour in the water, crumble in the stock cube, then stir in the tomatoes and bring to the boil. Stir to make sure the stock cube is dissolved, then add a little seasoning – mainly pepper at this stage. Stir in the chilli powder if used. Reduce the heat so that the mixture is just simmering and leave it to cook while you make the pancakes.

Heat a little oil or butter in a frying pan. Give the batter a good stir, adding a little extra milk to thin it down, and pour enough into the pan to coat the base fairly generously – the pancakes should not be too thin. Cook until the mixture is set and golden underneath, then turn the pancake over and cook the other side. When cooked, put on a warmed plate, lay a piece of absorbent kitchen paper on top, cover loosely with cooking foil and keep warm. Cook the remaining batter in the same way adding extra milk as necessary because the mixture will thicken on standing – you should have eight pancakes. Layer them with absorbent kitchen paper to prevent them from sticking together and keep the pancakes hot until they are all cooked.

For the topping, halve the avocados, remove their stones and scoop out the flesh, cutting it into chunks. Sprinkle the lemon juice over them, then stir in the garlic and cream.

Fill the pancakes with the meat mixture, fold them in half, and arrange them in a large warmed serving dish. Spoon the avocado mixture down the middle and sprinkle with the coriander. Serve at once. **Serves 4 to 6**

Lamb Pasties

(Illustrated on pages 106/107)

These tiny puff pastry triangles make an excellent cocktail snack. With their filling of minced lamb, feta cheese, olives and herbs, they offer a hint of Greek cooking. Serve them hot from the oven or warm.

350 g/12 oz minced lamb
2 cloves garlic, peeled and
  crushed
50 g/2 oz stuffed green olives,
  sliced
175 g/6 oz feta cheese, crumbled
2 teaspoons marjoram

1 small onion, peeled and finely
  chopped
salt and freshly ground black
  pepper
1 (397-g/13-oz) packet frozen
  puff pastry, thawed
1 egg, beaten

To prepare the filling, mix the lamb with the garlic, olives and feta, add the marjoram and onion and stir in plenty of seasoning. Mix the ingredients thoroughly to make sure that the meat is thoroughly broken up and that the cheese is evenly distributed.

Roll out the pastry on a lightly floured surface to a square slightly larger than 45-cm/18-in. It should be fairly thin. Trim off the edges neatly to give a 45-cm/18-in square, cut the pastry into six strips then cut across the strips in six parallel lines to make 36 small squares.

Brush the edges of each square of pastry with a little beaten egg then put a little of the filling mixture in the middle. Fold the pastry over the filling, sealing opposite corners together to make a small triangular pasty. Place the pasties on baking trays, brush them with a little egg and cook in a hot oven (220 C, 425 F, gas 7) for 20 to 25 minutes. When cooked the pastry should be well puffed and golden brown. Remove the pasties from the baking trays and cool them slightly on a wire rack, or serve at once on a warmed serving platter. **Makes 36**

119

Raised Pork Pie

This is not the easiest of pastry recipes to tackle, but the result justifies the effort involved. Once you have made hot-water crust pastry a few times you will find the task less daunting. Pork pie is excellent for including in a picnic meal or as part of a summer buffet.

1 kg/2 lb minced pork
1 onion, peeled and finely
  chopped
2 tablespoons chopped fresh
  sage
1 tablespoon juniper berries,
  finely crushed
salt and freshly ground black
  pepper

4 tablespoons brandy or dry
  sherry
Hot-water crust pastry
450 g/1 lb plain flour
$\frac{1}{2}$ teaspoon salt
175 g/6 oz lard or margarine
5 tablespoons milk
5 tablespoons water

To prepare the filling, mix the pork with all the other ingredients, making sure the meat is well broken up and all the ingredients evenly combined. Set aside while you prepare the pastry.

Sift the flour and salt into a bowl and make a well in the centre. Put the fat in a saucepan with the milk and water. Heat gently until the fat melts, then increase the heat to the hottest setting and bring quickly to the boil. Immediately the liquid boils pour it into the dry ingredients, quickly mix in the flour, then use your hands to knead the dough together until smooth – take care as it will be very hot. Cut two-thirds of the dough off to line the tin then cover the smaller portion with cling film and leave it in the bowl over a saucepan of hot water.

Grease an 18-cm/7-in loose-bottomed cake tin. Working fairly quickly, knead the dough to make a smooth ball then roll it out into a circle large enough to line the tin. Lift the pastry into the tin, holding the edge of the circle round the top of the tin. Carefully mould the pastry into the tin, making sure that you keep a good edge at the top. Press the pork mixture into the tin.

Roll out the reserved pastry to make a lid then lift it over the pie and mould the edges together well to seal in the filling. Trim off any excess with a pair of kitchen scissors and use the trimmings to make pastry leaves to decorate the top of the pie. Flute the edge of the pastry between your fingers. Cut a small hole in the middle to allow the steam to escape, then glaze the top with a little beaten egg and bake in a moderate oven (180 C, 350 F, gas 5) for $1\frac{1}{2}$ hours. Allow the cooked pie to cool in the tin then carefully push it out from the base. **Serves 8**

Picnic Pie

*This is another of those old favourite recipes that is infrequently cooked
these days. Even though it was originally meant for picnics there is no
reason why you shouldn't serve it with chipped potatoes (or a deliciously
crisp and fresh salad if you are conscious of your diet) or baked potatoes for
a good, hearty dinner. Again, it's the sort of recipe which will look very well
on a cold buffet table or it can be used as a good lunch-box bite. But however
you intend serving it, do try it as it's well worth the effort.*

1 quantity shortcrust pastry (see
   Veal and Ham Pie page 112)
beaten egg to glaze
Filling
1 kg/2 lb minced pork
1 large onion, peeled and very
   finely chopped or minced
1 teaspoon rubbed sage

4 tablespoons chopped parsley
salt and freshly ground black
   pepper
generous dash of Worcestershire
   sauce
2 teaspoons anchovy essence
3 hard-boiled eggs

Make up the pastry according to the recipe instructions, wrap it in cling
film and set it aside while you prepare the filling. Put the pork in a large
bowl with the onion, add all the remaining ingredients except the eggs
and mix thoroughly.

Roll out three-quarters of the pastry and use it to line a 1-kg/2-lb loaf
tin. Thoroughly grease the tin, lining the base with greaseproof paper
first if you have any fears that the pie will stick. Lift the pastry into the
tin, making the corners as neat as possible and keeping enough pastry
at the top to form a good edge. Put half the meat mixture into the pastry
case and press it down well. Lay the hard-boiled eggs on top, running
them down the length of the pie so that they will slice neatly as it is cut.
Carefully put the remaining meat mixture on top, piling it up slightly in
the middle.

Roll out the remaining pastry to make a lid. Dampen the edge of the
pastry base and put the lid on top, pressing it around the meat. Pinch
the edges together and cut off any excess, reserving it to decorate the
pie. Flute the edge between your fingers, then cut a small hole in the
middle of the lid to let the air escape. Roll out the trimmings and cut out
leaves or other shapes to decorate the pie. Stick these on top with a little
of the beaten egg for glazing, then brush all over the top of the pie with
a little egg so that it browns evenly.

Stand the pie on a Swiss roll tin or similar to catch any juices which
leak out and bake in a moderate oven (180 C, 350 F, gas 5) for $1\frac{1}{2}$ hours or
until the pastry is golden. Check occasionally during cooking and
brush a little extra egg on top. Allow the pie to cool in the tin then turn
it out and serve sliced. **Serves 8**

Cumberland Pork Pie

This juicy good-to-eat pie is topped with a rich cream-cheese pastry which makes a change from the usual shortcrust. You can always substitute bought puff pastry if you want to avoid making your own.

1 small onion, peeled and finely chopped
2 tablespoons oil
675 g/1½ lb minced pork
salt and freshly ground black pepper
2 tablespoons plain flour
grated rind and juice of 1 orange

450 ml/¾ pint dry red wine
2 tablespoons redcurrant jelly
Pastry
175 g/6 oz self-raising flour
50 g/2 oz butter
75 g/3 oz cream cheese
2 tablespoons water
beaten egg to glaze

Fry the onion in the oil until soft but not browned. Add the pork with plenty of seasoning and continue to cook, breaking up the meat with a wooden spoon, until the meat is lightly browned. Stir in the flour, orange rind and juice and wine, then add the redcurrant jelly and bring to the boil, stirring all the time. Remove the pan from the heat and set it aside.

To make the pastry, sift the flour into a bowl then add the butter and rub it in until the mixture resembles fine breadcrumbs. Add the cream cheese and mix it in well (use a fork or knife) then sprinkle in the water, gently knead the dough together and turn it out on to a lightly floured surface.

Have ready a 1.15-litre/2-pint pie dish. Roll out the pastry to about 5 cm/2 in larger than its top, cut a 2.5-cm/1-in strip from the edge then dampen the rim of the dish and press the strip of pastry on to it. Turn the filling into the dish, dampen the pastry edge, put the lid on top and press the edge together well to seal in the filling. Make a small hole in the middle of the pie, trim off any excess pastry and reserve for decorations. Knock up the edges of the pastry by tapping them gently with the blunt edge of a knife while holding the pastry rim in place with your left-hand index finger. Roll out the trimmings, cut out decorative shapes and secure them to the pie with beaten egg.

Brush the top with the beaten egg and bake the pie in a moderately hot oven (200 C, 400 F, gas 6) for 40 to 45 minutes or until the pastry is cooked through and golden brown on top. Serve at once. **Serves 4**

Pork and Beetroot Pie

This is a richly filled pie which should be served piping hot. Boiled new potatoes or creamed potatoes would make an excellent accompaniment along with some simply cooked green vegetables.

25 g/1 oz butter
1 large onion, peeled and
  chopped
450 g/1 lb uncooked beetroot,
  peeled and diced
450 g/1 lb minced pork
salt and freshly ground black
  pepper

1 chicken stock cube
300 ml/$\frac{1}{2}$ pint red wine
Shortcrust pastry
225 g/8 oz plain flour
100 g/4 oz margarine
about 4 tablespoons cold water
150 ml/$\frac{1}{4}$ pint soured cream to
  serve

Melt the butter in a frying pan and cook the onion and beetroot until the onion is soft but not browned. Stir in the pork and fry briefly, stirring all the time until the meat is well broken up. Add seasoning to taste and crumble in the stock cube. Pour in the wine, bring to the boil and remove from the heat.

Sift the flour into a bowl then add the fat, cut into small pieces, and rub in with your fingers until the mixture resembles fine breadcrumbs. Stir in just enough water to make a short dough, knead together lightly and roll out to give a piece large enough to cover a 1.15-litre/2-pint pie dish, with about 5 cm/2 in to spare all round the edge. Cut a narrow strip from the edge of the pastry and stick this to the edge of the dish with a little water.

Put the meat mixture into the pie dish then dampen the pastry edge and lift the lid over the pie. Press the edges together well to seal in the filling. Use a small round cutter (about 2.5 cm/1 in. in diameter) to cut a hole in the middle of the pie. Trim the pastry edges and flute them between your fingers. Roll out any trimmings to make leaves or petals to decorate the pie, and cut a circle of pastry about 3.5 cm/1$\frac{1}{2}$ in. in diameter from the scraps. Place this loosely over the hole. Glaze the pie with the beaten egg and bake in a moderately hot oven (200 C, 400 F, gas 6) for 40 minutes.

Carefully lift the circle of pastry from the middle of the pie. Use a funnel to pour in the soured cream, then replace the pastry circle and serve the pie at once. **Serves 4**

Pork and Apple Plait

(Illustrated on pages 106/107)

Not only does this pastry-covered pork mixture taste good, it also looks attractive enough to serve for a buffet party or on a rather special picnic. If you are serving the pastry hot, then make a sauce to go with it – try Mushroom Sauce (see page 162) or Red Wine Sauce (page 164) – alternatively offer a fairly moist vegetable dish with the plait.

Shortcrust pastry
275 g/10 oz plain flour
150 g/5 oz margarine or half and
   half lard and margarine
about 4 tablespoons water
Filling
450 g/1 lb minced pork
1 small onion, peeled and
   chopped

225 g/8 oz cooking apples,
   peeled, cored and cut into
   chunks
2 tablespoons wholegrain
   mustard
$\frac{1}{2}$ teaspoon rubbed sage
salt and freshly ground black
   pepper
beaten egg to glaze

To make the pastry, sift the flour into a bowl, add the fat, cut into small pieces, and rub it into the flour until the mixture resembles fine breadcrumbs. Sprinkle the water over the mixture, stirring it together with a round-bladed knife, and when the mixture clumps together, gather it with your fingers and knead it gently into a ball.

Mix together all the ingredients for the filling, making sure the apple is well dispersed and that the meat is thoroughly broken up. On a lightly floured surface, roll out the pastry to give an oblong shape measuring about 30 × 35 cm/12 × 14 in. Lift the pastry on to a large baking tray or roasting tin, lay the meat down the middle, then brush the edges with a little of the beaten egg for glazing. Cut the sides of the pastry into 2.5-cm/1-in wide strips, cutting in almost as far as the meat and at an angle, and fold the strips over the filling, alternating from side to side to make a top which looks like a plait. Brush with beaten egg and bake in a moderately hot oven (200 C, 400 F, gas 6) for about 45 minutes or until golden brown and cooked through. Use two large fish slices to transfer the plait to a serving platter, or cut it into slices first. **Serves 6**

Opposite page *Top: Spinach Kofta Pullao (page 133); Below: Ratatouille Beef Ring (page 132)* **Overleaf** *Clockwise from top right: Ravioli (page 138), Lasagne al Forno (page 135) and Tagliatelle with Veal and Dolcelatte Cream (page 136)*

Spicy Cornbread Pizza

(Illustrated on page 105)

*Fine cornmeal (or maize meal) is available from most health-food shops.
Red kidney beans, conjured into a simple savoury accompaniment, go well
with the pizza, and I have included a note at the end of the recipe to give you
some ideas. Offer a good and crisp green salad too.*

450 g/1 lb minced pork
1 tablespoons paprika
1 tablespoon ground coriander
salt and freshly ground black
  pepper
2 cloves garlic, peeled and
  crushed
1 bunch spring onions, chopped
50 g/2 oz stoned black olives

2 tomatoes, peeled
100 g/4 oz mozzarella cheese
Cornbread base
175 g/6 oz fine cornmeal
50 g/2 oz self-raising flour
2 teaspoons baking powder
½ teaspoon salt
about 150 ml/¼ pint milk

Put the pork in a bowl and add the paprika, coriander and seasoning to
taste. Thoroughly mix in the garlic and spring onions, then set the
mixture aside. Cut the olives in half and the tomatoes into quarters.
Slice the mozzarella cheese, then cut the slices into fine strips.

For the base, put the cornmeal and flour in a bowl, add the baking
powder and mix well with the salt. Make a well in the centre of the dry
ingredients, then pour in the milk and gradually mix them together to
make a fairly sticky dough. Turn the dough out on to a lightly floured
surface, knead it together well, press it into a 23-cm/9-in round and
place it on a greased baking tray. Pinch the edges up slightly to form a
rim.

Top the pizza base with the meat mixture, putting it on in small
lumps and piling it up in the middle. Do not bind the meat together or
press it down. Add the tomatoes and olives in between and on top of the
meat, then sprinkle the cheese over right at the end. Bake in a hot oven
(220 C, 425 F, gas 7) for 40 to 45 minutes until golden and cooked
through. Serve immediately. **Serves 4**

Quick Bean Pot
Fry 1 large chopped onion in a knob of butter until well softened but
not browned. Add plenty of seasoning and 1 (397-g/14-oz) can
chopped tomatoes and 2 (425-g/15-oz) cans red kidney beans (drained).
Bring to the boil then stir in plenty of chopped parsley and cook for 1
minute. Serve turned into a bowl and topped with several knobs of
butter if you like.

Left: Ravioli Rounds (page 139); Right: Macaroni Bake (page 141)

Spinach Pancake and Pork Layer

(Illustrated on page 108)

1 onion, peeled and finely
   chopped
25 g/1 oz butter
450 g/1 lb minced pork
225 g/8 oz button mushrooms,
   sliced
300 ml/½ pint full-bodied red
   wine
salt and freshly ground black
   pepper
Pancake batter
100 g/4 oz plain flour

3 eggs
150 ml/¼ pint milk
2 tablespoons water
1 (227-g/8-oz) packet frozen
   chopped spinach, thawed
oil for cooking
Topping
1 clove garlic, peeled and
   crushed
225 g/8 oz cream cheese
4 tablespoons sesame seeds
50 g/2 oz Cheddar cheese, grated

Fry the onion in the butter until soft but not browned. Add the pork and cook until lightly browned, stirring all the time to break up the meat as it cooks. Add the mushrooms and stir well, then pour in the wine and add seasoning to taste. Bring to the boil, cover the pan and simmer for 40 minutes.

To make the pancakes, sift the flour into a bowl and add a pinch of salt. Make a well in the middle and break the eggs into it. Pour in the milk, beating all the time and gradually working in the flour to make a smooth batter. Beat in the water. Thoroughly drain the spinach, squeezing out all the liquid, then add to the batter and stir well.

Heat a little oil in a large frying pan – make sure that the pan is one which is suitable for cooking pancakes and not one which will stick and burn particularly easily. Wipe the pan with a pad of absorbent kitchen paper to remove any excess oil then pour in enough batter to cover the base of the pan. Tilt the pan as you pour in the batter so that it spreads out and makes a thin, even coating. Cook until the underneath of the pancake is browned, then use a large fish slice to turn the pancake over and cook the other side until golden. Remove the pancake from the pan and cook the remaining batter in the same way. Lay pieces of absorbent kitchen paper between the cooked pancakes to prevent them from sticking together.

When all the pancakes are cooked, beat the garlic into the cheese for the topping, then stir in the sesame seeds. Lay a pancake on a large flat fireproof platter or shallow dish. Top with a thin covering of the freshly cooked meat, then add a second pancake. Continue layering the pancakes and the meat in this way until all are used. Spread the cream cheese mixture thickly over the top and sprinkle with the Cheddar, then put the pancakes under a hot grill until golden and bubbling. Serve at once, cutting the pancakes into wedges at the table. **Serves 4**

RICE AND PASTA

Minced meats and pasta are a traditional partnership in many famous dishes from the heart of Europe, and rice also marries well with mince in a collection of easy, economical recipes – many of which offer a taste of the exotic. Often, just a simple salad and some fresh crusty bread is all that's needed to complete these dishes – try some of them and you may find that they become firm favourites with the whole family.

Chicken Cannelloni

The combination of minced chicken and chopped chicken livers makes a full-flavoured and rich filling for the pasta tubes. Red Wine Sauce (see page 164) can be substituted for the Tomato Sauce if you wish.

8 cannelloni tubes
salt and freshly ground black
  pepper
oil for cooking
450 g/1 lb minced chicken
100 g/4 oz chicken livers, finely
  chopped
4 tablespoons chopped parsley
4 spring onions, finely chopped

50 g/2 oz fresh breadcrumbs
2 tablespoons brandy
1 quantity Rich Tomato Sauce
  (page 163)
Topping
50 g/2 oz fresh breadcrumbs
4 tablespoons grated Parmesan
  cheese

Cook the cannelloni in plenty of boiling salted water, with a little oil added, for about 15 minutes or until the pasta is just tender. Drain immediately, then rinse the tubes under cold running water and leave to dry on absorbent kitchen paper.

Mix the chicken with the chicken livers, seasoning, parsley, spring onions and breadcrumbs then stir in the brandy. Make sure all the ingredients are thoroughly combined.

Fill the pasta tubes with the chicken mixture, pressing it in well, and arrange them in a buttered ovenproof dish. Make up the sauce according to the recipe instructions and pour it evenly over the pasta. Cover with cooking foil and cook in a moderately hot oven (200 C, 400 F, gas 6) for 40 minutes then uncover the dish and sprinkle first the breadcrumbs and then the Parmesan over the pasta. Return to the oven for a further 15 minutes or until lightly browned on top, and serve immediately. **Serves 4**

Ratatouille Beef Ring

(Illustrated on page 125)

*This recipe makes a complete light meal needing no accompaniment –
cooked rice and beef go to make up the outer ring while the ratatouille is a
moist vegetable filling.*

100 g/4 oz long-grain rice
1 beef stock cube
300 ml/½ pint water
25 g/1 oz butter
1 large onion, peeled and
  chopped
450 g/1 lb minced beef
100 g/4 oz carrots, diced
2 tablespoons chopped parsley
salt and freshly ground black
  pepper
1 egg, beaten

Ratatouille
1 large aubergine
2 courgettes
1 red or green pepper
150 ml/¼ pint olive oil
1 large clove garlic, peeled and
  crushed
1 large onion, peeled and
  chopped
450 g/1 lb tomatoes, peeled (page
  144) and quartered
salt and freshly ground black
  pepper
plenty of chopped parsley

Put the rice in a saucepan and crumble in the stock cube then pour in
the water and bring to the boil. Cover the pan, reduce the heat and
simmer for 25 minutes or until all the stock has been absorbed and the
grains are tender.

While the rice is cooking prepare the aubergine for the ratatouille for
the ring. Cut the stalk off, trim off the opposite end and cut the
aubergine into bite-sized chunks. Place these in a colander and sprinkle
them fairly generously with salt. Set aside over a bowl and leave for 30
minutes.

Melt the butter in a frying pan and fry the onion until soft but not
browned. Remove the pan from the heat and stir in the beef. Add the
carrots, parsley and seasoning to taste, then mix in the beaten egg and
the cooked rice. Thoroughly grease a 1.15-litre/2-pint ring tin and
press the mixture into it. Stand the tin on a baking tray and cook in a
moderately hot oven (200 C, 400 F, gas 6) for 30 minutes.

Meanwhile prepare the ratatouille. Wash the aubergine pieces
thoroughly and drain, then dry them on absorbent kitchen paper. Very
lightly peel the courgettes and slice them. Cut the stalk end off the
pepper, remove all the seeds and pith from inside, wash the pepper
shell then dry thoroughly and cut into thin slices. Heat about half the
oil in a large frying pan and add the aubergine. Cook, turning
frequently, for a few minutes. Add the remaining oil and stir in the
garlic, onion and pepper then cook until the onion is soft. Stir in
seasoning to taste and continue to cook until the aubergines are tender.

Lastly add the tomatoes to cook until they are quite soft but not broken down completely. Stir in the parsley.

To serve, turn the ring out on to a heated serving dish and fill the middle with the ratatouille mixture. Serve any extra ratatouille separately. **Serves 4**

Spaghetti Bolognaise

(Illustrated on page 145)

The bolognaise sauce in this recipe can be served with different sorts of pasta – noodles or shapes. It can also be used in a lasagne or to layer with pasta shapes in a baked dish.

1 large green pepper
4 tablespoons olive oil
100 g/4 oz carrots, diced
1 large onion, peeled and chopped
2 cloves garlic, peeled and crushed
350 g/12 oz minced beef
350 g/12 oz minced pork
2 tablespoons plain flour
450 ml/$\frac{3}{4}$ pint full-bodied red wine

1 beef stock cube
1 (397-g/14-oz) can chopped tomatoes
2 tablespoons tomato purée
1 teaspoon marjoram
generous pinch of thyme
100 g/4 oz mushrooms, sliced
350 g/12 oz spaghetti
salt
freshly grated Parmesan cheese

Cut the pepper in half, remove the stalk and all the pith and seeds from inside and chop the flesh. Heat the oil in a heavy-based saucepan, add the pepper, carrots, onion and garlic, and fry, stirring all the time, until the onion is soft but not brown. Add both types of mince to the pan and cook, breaking up the meat with a wooden spoon, until evenly browned. Stir in the flour and pour in the wine, crumble the stock cube into the pan and stir in the tomatoes. Add the tomato purée and herbs and bring to the boil. Stir thoroughly to make sure the stock cube has dissolved then reduce the heat and simmer, covered, for 45 minutes. Add the mushrooms to the pan after 30 minutes cooking time.

Cook the spaghetti in plenty of boiling salted water with a little oil added for 15 to 20 minutes. Drain it thoroughly and divide it between individual heated plates. Ladle the sauce over the spaghetti and top each portion with some Parmesan cheese. Serve immediately. **Serves 4**

Spinach Kofta Pullao

(Illustrated on page 125)

This spicy mixture of rice and spinach cooked with beef meatballs makes a meal in itself. Serve a selection of side dishes with it if you like – for example try Cucumber Raita (see page 90), crisp popadums, roughly chopped hard-boiled eggs, tomatoes with chopped spring onions and a pickle such as mango pickle.

Kofta
450 g/1 lb minced beef
50 g/2 oz fresh breadcrumbs
salt and freshly ground black pepper
1 clove garlic, peeled and crushed
2 teaspoons ground fenugreek
2 teaspoons chilli powder
2 teaspoons ground coriander
1 egg, beaten
Pullao
1 large onion, peeled and sliced

50 g/2 oz ghee or butter
1 cinnamon stick
bay leaf
4 green cardamoms
1 tablespoon cumin seeds (the black cumin seeds called *kala jeera* are best if you can find them)
4 cloves
225 g/8 oz basmati rice
450 ml/$\frac{3}{4}$ pint water
450 g/1 lb fresh spinach, trimmed

To make the kofta, mix the beef with the breadcrumbs, seasoning, garlic and spices. Stir in the egg and mix thoroughly. Shape the mixture into sixteen meatballs.

For the pullao, separate the onion slices into rings. Heat the ghee or butter in a flameproof casserole or heavy-based saucepan and fry the meatballs, turning frequently, until browned all over. Remove them from the pan and set them aside.

Add the onion rings, cinnamon and bay leaf to the oil remaining in the pan. Stir in the cardamoms, cumin and cloves and cook over a medium heat for 5 minutes.

While the spices are cooking wash the rice (see page 91), add it with a good pinch of salt to the spices in the pan and pour in the water. Bring to the boil and give the rice a stir, then reduce the heat so that the liquid is just simmering, put a lid on the pan and cook gently for 10 minutes.

Wash and thoroughly drain the spinach and roughly shred it. Add it to the half-cooked rice and stir lightly, then put in the kofta and replace the lid. Cook at a simmer for a further 10 minutes then uncover the pan and cook for a final 5 minutes. By now all the excess liquid should have evaporated to leave a moist pullao. Lightly fork the ingredients together and serve at once. **Serves 4**

Lasagne al Forno

(Illustrated on pages 126/127)

I always find that we can eat far more of this dish than I anticipate. With a green salad (see page 172), the baked lasagne makes a delicious meal – moist, well flavoured and offering a good balance of texture.

2 tablespoons olive oil
2 cloves garlic, peeled and
  crushed
1 large onion, peeled and
  chopped
450 g/1 lb minced beef
salt and freshly ground black
  pepper
2 tablespoons plain flour
300 ml/$\frac{1}{2}$ pint red wine
1 (397-g/14-oz) can chopped
  tomatoes

100 g/4 oz button mushrooms,
  chopped
1 teaspoon marjoram
350 g/12 oz lasagne
Topping
1 quantity Béchamel Sauce (page
  162)
50 g/2 oz Cheddar cheese, grated
2 tablespoons grated Parmesan
  cheese

Heat the oil in a flameproof casserole or heavy-based saucepan. Add the garlic and onion and cook until the onion is soft but not browned. Stir in the meat and add seasoning to taste and cook until the meat is well browned all over. Add the flour and stir well then pour in the wine and tomatoes and bring to the boil. Add the mushrooms and marjoram, reduce the heat and simmer gently, with the lid on the pan, for 30 minutes.

Meanwhile, prepare the béchamel sauce according to the recipe instructions. Cook the lasagne in plenty of boiling salted water with a little oil added to stop the sheets sticking together for about 15 minutes or until just tender, drain thoroughly and rinse the strips under cold water. Lay them out on absorbent kitchen paper to dry.

Layer the pasta and meat sauce in a large lasagne dish starting and ending with the pasta, and making sure that there is plenty of pasta between the meat layers. Top with the béchamel sauce and sprinkle the Cheddar over. Finally add the Parmesan and bake the lasagne in a moderately hot oven (200 C, 400 F, gas 6) for about 40 minutes or until the top is golden and crusty. Serve at once. **Serves 4 to 6**

Tagliatelle with Veal and Dolcelatte Cream

(Illustrated on pages 126/127)

Creamy dolcelatte cheese perfectly complements the simply cooked minced veal in this sauce. Serve the noodles in bowls and offer a green salad with the pasta. Some crusty bread would also go down very well.

2 tablespoons olive oil
450 g/1 lb minced veal
1 clove garlic, peeled and
 crushed
100 g/4 oz button mushrooms,
 sliced
1 (227-g/8-oz) can pimentos,
 drained and sliced

150 ml/$\frac{1}{4}$ pint single cream
225 g/8 oz dolcelatte cheese, cut
 into cubes
salt and freshly ground black
 pepper
450 g/1 lb tagliatelle verde

Heat the oil (you can use a different oil instead of olive oil if you prefer) in a large frying pan. Add the veal and the garlic and cook, breaking up the meat with a wooden spoon, until lightly browned all over. Stir in the mushrooms and pimentos, then pour in the cream and add the dolcelatte. Season with plenty of black pepper and a little salt. Leave over a *very* low heat so that the cream warms through and the cheese melts, but do not allow the mixture to boil.

Cook the tagliatelle in boiling salted water with a little oil added for about 15 minutes. When cooked the pasta should be 'al dente' (tender but still with a bit of bite). Drain immediately or it will continue to cook.

If the frying pan containing the meat mixture is large enough, turn the noodles into it and mix well, otherwise, return the noodles to the saucepan and pour the meat sauce over them. Mix lightly and ladle the pasta into bowls to serve. **Serves 4**

Pasta Timbale

If you are bored with preparing the same old lasagne dish time and time again, then try this for a change. Surprisingly, it takes less effort than lasagne, which is layered with cooked sauces, because the filling only needs to be thoroughly mixed before the ingredients can be assembled and baked.

450 g/1 lb lasagne verde
salt and freshly ground black
  pepper
225 g/8 oz minced veal
225 g/8 oz minced pork
1 large onion, peeled and
  chopped
2 tablespoons oil
2 cloves garlic, peeled and
  crushed

50 g/2 oz fresh breadcrumbs
1 egg, beaten
225 g/8 oz Ricotta cheese
3 tablespoons chopped fresh
  basil or 1 tablespoon dried
  basil
1 quantity Rich Tomato Sauce
  (page 163) to serve

Cook the lasagne in plenty of boiling salted water with a little oil added for 10 minutes; it should be not quite cooked. Drain and rinse under cold water then lay the pieces out on absorbent kitchen paper. If you do not have a very large saucepan, you may have to cook the lasagne in two batches.

Mix both types of mince in a bowl. Heat the oil in a frying pan and cook the onion and garlic until the onion is soft but not browned. Add the onion to the bowl and mix in all the remaining ingredients including seasoning to taste.

Thoroughly grease a 1-kg/2-lb loaf tin (if you think it may stick, line the base with a piece of greaseproof paper first). Line the loaf tin completely with lasagne, making sure it overlaps at the edges and hangs over the sides of the tin. Press a layer of the meat mixture around the pasta to cover it completely and evenly. Put another layer of pasta in the tin to completely cover the meat (both sides and base), and overlap the pasta to make sure it forms a complete layer. Put the rest of the meat mixture into the tin and press it down, then fold the ends of the lasagne over the meat and lay any remaining pieces of lasagne across the top.

Stand the tin in a roasting tin and pour in boiling water around it to half way up the sides of the outer tin. Cover the loaf tin with a piece of greased cooking foil, sealing it down tightly on the rim of the tin and bake the timbale in a moderate oven (180 C, 350 F, gas 4) for $1\frac{1}{2}$ hours. Meanwhile make the tomato sauce according to the recipe instructions or heat it through if already prepared.

To serve, turn out on to a warmed serving dish and serve at once, with the tomato sauce. **Serves 6**

Ravioli

(Illustrated on pages 126/127)

Most people are put off the idea of making their own ravioli because it involves preparing your own pasta dough. But making pasta, although not simple, is not really difficult either – it just requires a little care. This is not the sort of recipe you can knock together in a hurry, but homemade pasta tastes quite different to the dried type, and freshly made ravioli really is delicious.

Filling
100 g/4 oz minced pork
100 g/4 oz minced veal
1 small onion, peeled and very
    finely chopped or grated
1 teaspoon concentrated tomato
    purée
25 g/1 oz fresh breadcrumbs
generous pinch of ground mace
generous pinch of thyme
1 teaspoon marjoram
2 tablespoons dry sherry or
    vermouth
salt and freshly ground black
    pepper
Pasta dough
225 g/8 oz strong plain flour
salt
2 large eggs
3 tablespoons olive oil
beaten egg to seal
To serve
1 quantity Rich Tomato Sauce
    (page 163)
freshly grated Parmesan cheese

Make the filling first so that it is ready as soon as the pasta is rolled out. Mix all the ingredients together thoroughly, making sure the mixture is well seasoned.

Now make the pasta dough. Sift the flour into a bowl and add a very generous pinch of salt. Make a well in the middle and break in the eggs. Pour the oil over the eggs, then beat them with a wooden spoon. Gradually work in the flour, pounding the mixture with the wooden spoon to help it bind together. The mixture will appear quite stiff. When it starts to clump together, scrape all the bits off the wooden spoon and use your hand to knead it into a dough.

Turn the dough out on to a very lightly floured surface (use as little flour as possible) and knead it thoroughly until it becomes smooth and softer. This will take some time but the dough must be smooth and pliable before you roll it out. If you have a pasta machine, roll the dough between the rollers on the widest setting several times, gradually reducing the space between the rollers.

When the pasta is smooth cut it in half and wrap one half in cling film to prevent it drying out. Lightly flour the work surface and roll the other piece of dough into an oblong shape. Try to keep the shape as neat as possible as you roll the dough, lifting it off the work surface occasionally and turning it round. Keep the surface lightly floured but use the minimum. (I find it easier just at the beginning of rolling if the dough adheres to the surface very slightly.) Roll the dough gradually, lifting it off the surface frequently and turning it round to keep the shape even. Do not turn the dough over during rolling and keep the pin very lightly dusted with flour. I find it easier if I can allow about half of the rolled dough to hang down off the work surface as I roll away from it; this gives extra weight to prevent the pasta from slipping. If you roll the pasta in short bursts it should not split. The final rolled-out oblong should measure about 25 × 42 cm/10 × 17 in, though if you can make it thinner, do. If the edges are very uneven trim them slightly but if you have kept the shape fairly well there should be no need to cut any off. Make sure the work surface under the pasta is lightly floured, then cover it with cling film to stop it drying out. If you are short of space for rolling out the second portion of dough, roll up the first piece with the cling film inside like a Swiss roll then wrap the whole thing in cling film.

When both pieces of pasta are rolled, take small spoonfuls of the meat mixture and dot them on to one piece in straight lines with about 3.5 cm/1$\frac{1}{2}$ in between each mound (aim for about 28 mounds, with small, even gaps between each). Brush between the meat with beaten egg then carefully lift the second sheet of pasta over the top. Working from one end, press the pasta together between the mounds of meat, pushing out all the air as you go along. Make sure the pasta is well sealed to keep the filling in, then cut in straight lines between the filling to give small, neat squares. Cover the ravioli with a piece of cling film. Prepare the tomato sauce according to the recipe instructions or heat it through if already prepared. Bring a large saucepan of salted water to the boil, adding a little oil to stop the water from frothing up, then lower the ravioli one by one into the boiling water and bring back to the boil. Reduce the heat so that the water is just boiling and cook for 10 to 15 minutes.

Drain the cooked pasta immediately and turn it into a serving bowl. Pour the tomato sauce over and sprinkle with grated Parmesan. Serve immediately. **Serves 4**

Ravioli Rounds *(Illustrated on page 128)*
Make the pasta as in the main recipe. Omit the minced pork from the filling and substitute 100 g/4 oz ricotta cheese, mixing it with the minced veal. Cut 5-cm/2-in circles from the rolled-out pasta, place a little of the filling on each and brush the edge of the pasta with beaten egg. Fold in half, pinching the edges together to seal the filling in a small pastry shape. Cook in boiling water as above, then serve with garlic butter, chopped basil and grated Parmesan cheese.

Gala Pilaf

(Illustrated on page 145)

This is a rich rice dish which is spiced with sweet curry spices and cooked in coconut milk. Mango, apricots and raisins mingle with green pistachio nuts to complete the exotic concoction and to complement the delicately scented basmati rice which dominates the pilaf.

100 g/4 oz desiccated coconut
600 ml/1 pint boiling water
2 onions, peeled and sliced
50 g/2 oz ghee (see below)
4 green cardamoms
1 tablespoon cumin seeds
1 cinnamon stick
2 cloves
bay leaf
1 clove garlic, peeled and crushed
450 g/1 lb minced lamb
275 g/10 oz basmati rice

salt and freshly ground black pepper
25 g/1 oz raisins
50 g/2 oz dried apricots, chopped (use the type which do not require pre-soaking)
1 mango (the fruit should be just ripe, but not too soft)
50 g/2 oz shelled pistachio nuts, roughly chopped
2 hard-boiled eggs, cut into wedges

First soak the coconut in the boiling water and leave until completely cooled. Strain the liquid and thoroughly squeeze the coconut to extract the last of the milk and set aside.

Separate the onion slices into rings and fry in the ghee until browned. Do this in a saucepan over a moderate heat, carefully turning the slices occasionally so that they cook evenly and slowly without burning. Remove about half the onion rings from the pan and set them aside on a piece of absorbent kitchen paper; they will be used to garnish the pilaf.

Add the spices, bay leaf and garlic to the pan and fry for a few minutes, stirring constantly. Stir in the lamb and cook until lightly browned, breaking it up with a wooden spoon to ensure even cooking.

Meanwhile wash the rice: put it in a bowl, pour in cold water and carefully swirl the grains with your fingers. Pour off the water, pour in fresh water, and continue in this way for about four changes of water, taking care not to handle the grains roughly or they will be damaged and become sticky when cooked. Drain thoroughly.

Add the rice to the pan with seasoning to taste. Make up the coconut milk to 600 ml/1 pint with extra milk if necessary, then pour it into the pan and bring to the boil. Lower the heat and put a lid on the pan, simmer gently for 15 minutes then remove the lid and sprinkle the raisins and apricots over the mixture, replacing the lid immediately. Do not stir the fruit into the rice. Continue cooking for another 15 to 20 minutes.

Meanwhile prepare the mango: use a small sharp knife to peel the fruit, then cut the flesh off the large central stone. Cut it away in chunks and cut any very large pieces into bite-sized portions. When the rice is cooked, carefully fork the cooked fruit into the pilaf, adding the mango and pistachios. Lightly mix in the eggs and garnish the pilaf with the reserved fried onion rings. Serve at once. **Serves 4**

Aubergine and Lamb Pilaf

Instead of the fruit in the above recipe, vegetables such as aubergines can be used for a delicious lamb pilaf. Omit the mango and apricots, use 1 large aubergine and cut it into small cubes. Soak these in salt for 30 minutes, rinse and dry them, then fry them with the spices and lamb. Substitute lightly toasted flaked almonds for the pistachio nuts and stir in 4 peeled, quartered tomatoes instead of the eggs. **Serves 4**

Note. Ghee is the Indian term for clarified butter. It is available in cans from Indian grocers and many delicatessens or you can make it yourself. To do this, melt 225 g/8 oz butter in a saucepan, simmer it gently for 30 minutes then strain through a piece of fine muslin, leaving the sediment in the bottom of the pan. Pour the fat into a container and allow it to cool. This will keep in the bottom of the refrigerator for a couple of months.

Macaroni Bake

(Illustrated on page 128)

2 tablespoons olive oil
2 cloves garlic, peeled and
  crushed
1 large onion, peeled and sliced
450 g/1 lb minced lamb
2 tablespoons plain flour
salt and freshly ground black
  pepper
1 (397-g/14-oz) can chopped
  tomatoes

100 g/4 oz button mushrooms,
  sliced
2 tablespoons chopped parsley
1 teaspoon marjoram
350 g/12 oz short-cut macaroni
4 tablespoons grated Parmesan
  cheese

Heat the oil in a large frying pan and cook the garlic and onion until the onion is soft but not browned. Stir in the meat and cook, breaking it up with a wooden spoon, until evenly browned. Add the flour and plenty of seasoning and continue to cook for a few minutes before stirring in the tomatoes and mushrooms. Stir the herbs into the meat then transfer it to an ovenproof dish.

    Cook the macaroni in plenty of boiling salted water with a little oil added for about 15 minutes or until soft. Drain immediately then turn into the dish on top of the meat mixture. Sprinkle the cheese on top and bake in a moderately hot oven (200 C, 400 F, gas 6) for 20 to 30 minutes or until well browned on top. Serve at once. **Serves 4**

Risotto

(Illustrated on pages 146/147)

A risotto is a rice dish which has lots of other ingredients cooked with it. Traditionally these should all be added at different stages as the rice cooks. Here is a basic recipe using minced pork, and you can expand it or alter it as you see fit; the only real rule being that when the dish is served it should be quite juicy and no one of the ingredients should be overcooked. If you are adding food that will be ready very quickly – canned artichoke hearts, button mushrooms or ripe olives, for example – then toss these into the rice at the last minute. If there are vegetables which need longer cooking – carrots, celery or celeriac, for example – then sauté them with the onions, garlic and rice at the beginning of the cooking.

I like to serve risotto straight from the pan (basic laziness, as I hate washing up) with plenty of Parmesan cheese and the ubiquitous green salad! It's good peasant-type food which is filling and quite delicious when well cooked.

1 large red pepper
1 large green pepper
4 tablespoons olive oil
1 large onion, peeled and chopped
2 cloves garlic, peeled and crushed
4 sticks celery, sliced
450 g/1 lb minced pork
225 g/8 oz long-grain rice

1 chicken stock cube
600 ml/1 pint water
salt and freshly ground black pepper
100 g/4 oz frozen French beans
4 tablespoons chopped fresh basil or marjoram
freshly grated Parmesan cheese to serve

Cut the peppers in half, remove stalks, seeds and pith, and chop the flesh. Heat the oil in a heavy-based saucepan and cook the peppers, onion and garlic until the onion is soft but not browned. Stir in the celery and meat and cook until the meat is lightly browned. Add the rice and fry until the grains begin to turn transparent. Crumble in the stock cube and stir well.

Taking great care, because the steam could scald you, pour the water into the pan. Add seasoning and bring to the boil. As soon as the liquid boils reduce the heat so that it simmers gently. Cover the pan and cook over a moderate heat for 10 minutes. Add the beans to the pan and bring back to the boil then re-cover the pan and cook for a further 10 to 15 minutes.

Just before serving the risotto, stir in the herb and fluff up the rice. Offer the Parmesan cheese separately. **Serves 4**

Fried Rice with Pork and Prawns

(Illustrated on page 148)

Oriental-style fried rice makes a good supper dish. Serve the rice straight from the pan or in one big serving bowl with small bowls and chopsticks for each person so that everyone dips into the pan of rice to take what they require. If you want to make the dish really economical, then omit the prawns and use button mushrooms instead of the Chinese dried mushrooms.

4 Chinese dried mushrooms	1 (227-g/8-oz) can water
4 tablespoons oil	chestnuts, drained and sliced
a few drops of sesame oil	4 tablespoons soy sauce
1 clove garlic, peeled and	450 ml/$\frac{3}{4}$ pint water
crushed	2 eggs, beaten
225 g/8 oz long-grain rice	225 g/8 oz peeled cooked prawns
450 g/1 lb minced pork	4 spring onions, shredded

Put the mushrooms in a small basin and pour in enough hot water to cover them. Put a saucer on top to keep them in the water and leave them to soak for 15 minutes.

Meanwhile, heat 3 tablespoons of the oil in a heavy-based saucepan or wok, add the sesame oil and garlic, then stir in the rice and stir-fry until the grains are transparent. Add the pork and continue to cook, stirring frequently, until the meat is lightly cooked.

While the pork is cooking, drain the mushrooms and slice them thinly. Add them to the pan with the water chestnuts and pour in the soy sauce. Stir in the water, then bring to the boil. Reduce the heat and cover the pan tightly then leave to simmer for 10 minutes.

Meanwhile heat the remaining 1 tablespoon oil in a large frying pan until really hot then pour in the beaten eggs and cook quickly until they are bubbling and begin to set. Lift the sides of this omelette to allow any uncooked egg to run on to the pan. When the omelette has completely set and the underneath is well browned, use a large fish slice to turn it over. If you are not confident that you can do this, then invert it on to a large plate and then slide it back into the pan. When cooked, slide the omelette out on to a plate lined with absorbent kitchen paper.

Add the prawns to the rice mixture but do not stir them in. Replace the lid on the pan and cook for a further 10 minutes. Cut the omelette first into thin strips, then across into 2.5 cm/1-in lengths. When the rice is cooked, fork the prawns, omelette pieces and spring onions into the grains and serve at once. **Serves 4**

Pasta Pork with Pine Nuts

(Illustrated on pages 146/147)

You can use any shape of pasta you like in this dish, but the longer shapes are better than the shells or bows. It will form a meal in itself with a light salad, or try the Tomato and Mozzarella Salad (see page 172) with it if you like.

2 tablespoons olive oil
2 cloves garlic, peeled and
  crushed
1 small onion, peeled and
  chopped
450 g/1 lb minced pork
salt and freshly ground black
  pepper

450 g/1 lb tomatoes, peeled (see
  below) and roughly chopped
4 tablespoons brandy
350 g/12 oz pasta spirals
50 g/2 oz pine nuts
2 tablespoons chopped fresh
  basil

Heat the oil in a flameproof casserole or heavy-based saucepan, add the garlic and onion then stir in the meat and cook until lightly browned. Add seasoning to taste and stir in the tomatoes. Pour in the brandy then reduce the heat so that the mixture is barely cooking. Put a lid on the pan and leave it to cook very very gently while the pasta is prepared.

Cook the pasta in plenty of boiling salted water with a little oil added for about 15 minutes or until the the pasta is 'al dente' – tender but not soft. Drain the pasta immediately then stir it into the meat and sprinkle in the pine nuts. Add the basil and serve at once. **Serves 4**

To Peel Tomatoes

Put the tomatoes in a large bowl then pour in freshly boiling water, making sure they are well covered, and leave for 30 to 60 seconds. The length of time will depend on how ripe the tomatoes are. If they are quite red, then they will peel quickly; if they are very pale they may need longer than suggested. Drain the tomatoes and use a pointed knife to make a small split in one place. The skin can then be peeled off easily.

Opposite page *Top: Spaghetti Bolognaise (page 134); Below: Gala Pilaf (page 140)* **Overleaf** *Clockwise from top right: Pasta Pork with Pine Nuts, Pork and Spinach Cannelloni with Vermouth Cream (page 150) and Risotto (page 142)*

Pork Pearls

(Illustrated opposite)

These are steamed meatballs which are coated in rice. The uncooked grains of rice cling to the raw meat and as the meatballs are steamed the grains cook and expand. Serve the pork pearls with some mixed stir-fried vegetables – Chinese cabbage, beansprouts, spring onions, sliced water chestnuts and bamboo shoots – to make a light main course. If you served Spring Rolls as a starter (see page 24), then the menu would be quite well balanced.

450 g/1 lb minced pork
½ teaspoon five-spice powder
2 tablespoons soy sauce
a few drops of sesame oil
1 egg, beaten

2 tablespoons dry sherry
225 g/8 oz long-grain rice (not
   easy-cook)
1 small cucumber to garnish

Mix with the pork with the five-spice powder, soy sauce, sesame oil and egg. Add the sherry and stir thoroughly to make sure that the spice is well mixed in. Take small spoonfuls of the mixture and shape each into a small ball about the size of a walnut – you should have 24 meatballs. Roll each meatball in the rice so that the grains stick to it, then place them on heatproof plates and cook them in a steamer over boiling water for 45 minutes. (You may have to ccok them in batches if you are unable to stack the plates in your steamer.) Keep the pork pearls hot, covered, in a cool oven until all are cooked.

For the garnish, very lightly peel the cucumber (you should remove only the tough part of the skin and leave a bright green covering). Trim the ends off, cut the cucumber into 7.5-cm/3-in lengths and slice each piece lengthways. Put the slices in a bowl with enough cold water to cover them and add some ice cubes. Leave for at least 30 minutes.

To serve, thoroughly drain the cucumber then toss the pieces together and arrange them on the edge of a large platter. Pile the pork pearls in the middle and serve. **Serves 4**

Top: Pork Pearls; Below: Fried Rice with Pork and Prawns (page 143)

Pork and Spinach Cannelloni with Vermouth Cream

(Illustrated on pages 146/147)

Cannelloni – pasta tubes – can be filled with a beef sauce if you prefer and served with Tomato Sauce (page 163) poured over. Alternatively the meat-filled pasta can be topped with Cheese Sauce (see page 162). This recipe is slightly more unusual and suited to special occasions.

8 cannelloni tubes
salt and freshly ground black
  pepper
Meat filling
2 tablespoons olive oil
1 large clove garlic, peeled and
  crushed
1 large onion, peeled and finely
  chopped
450 g/1 lb minced pork
1 (227-g/8-oz) packet frozen
  chopped spinach, thawed and
  thoroughly drained
50 g/2 oz fresh breadcrumbs

Vermouth cream
50 g/2 oz butter
1 small onion, peeled and finely
  chopped
2 tablespoons plain flour
1 chicken stock cube
300 ml/$\frac{1}{2}$ pint dry white
  vermouth
150 ml/$\frac{1}{4}$ pint single cream
Topping
25 g/1 oz fresh breadcrumbs
4 tablespoons grated Parmesan
  cheese
2 tablespoons chopped parsley

Cook the cannelloni in plenty of boiling salted water for about 15 minutes or until the pasta is just tender. Drain and rinse under cold water, then lay the pieces on absorbent kitchen paper to dry.

Heat the oil for the meat filling in a large frying pan and cook the garlic and onion until the onion is soft but not browned. Stir in the pork and cook, breaking up the meat, until lightly browned. Add the spinach and breadcrumbs and stir in seasoning to taste. Remove the pan from the heat.

To make the vermouth cream, melt the butter in a saucepan and fry the onion in it until very soft. Stir in the flour, crumble in the stock cube and add the vermouth, stirring all the time. Bring to the boil and cook for 2 minutes, then remove the pan from the heat and stir in the cream. Taste and adjust seasoning if necessary.

Fill the cannelloni with the pork and spinach mixture then lay the pieces in a buttered ovenproof dish. Pour the vermouth cream evenly over the pasta. Mix the topping ingredients and sprinkle them on top then cook in a moderately hot oven (200 C, 400 F, gas 6) for 30 to 40 minutes or until the topping is golden and crisp. Serve at once. **Serves 4**

SPECIAL-OCCASION MINCE

How often do you count the cost of entertaining in style and give a shudder of horror? If you're in the money and feel you can throw caution to the winds then forget about mince, but if you are planning a dinner party for which you don't really want to buy pounds of fillet steak, then try some of these ideas – they are not necessarily incredibly cheap, but they do compete well with recipes using ingredients in the upper end of the price range. Of course, if you really do want to go to town, take the recipe for steak tartare and serve it to a dinner party of four or more, but remember not everyone appreciates an uncooked dish!

Sherried Chicken Soufflé

Serve this soufflé as soon as it is cooked, with a crisp salad, lightly sautéed courgettes or some other crunchy vegetable.

1 onion, peeled and finely
   chopped
50 g/2 oz butter
50 g/2 oz plain flour
150 ml/¼ pint dry sherry
150 ml/¼ pint double cream
1 chicken stock cube

450 g/1 lb minced chicken
salt and freshly ground black
   pepper
a little freshly grated nutmeg
4 tablespoons chopped parsley
5 eggs, separated

Fry the onion in the butter until soft but not browned. Stir in the flour, then gradually stir in the sherry and cream and bring to the boil. Remove from the heat and allow to cool slightly. Crumble in the chicken stock cube and add the chicken. Season to taste. Add a little nutmeg and the parsley then beat in the egg yolks.

Whisk the egg whites until they stand in stiff peaks. Beat a couple of spoonfuls of the egg whites into the chicken mixture then carefully fold in the remainder. Turn the mixture into a large greased soufflé dish and bake in a moderate oven (180 C, 350 F, gas 5) for 50 to 55 minutes. When cooked, the soufflé should be risen and golden brown. **Serves 4 to 6**

Chicken Croquettes

(Illustrated on page 165)

I have included only a few recipes for minced chicken but this is one of those which I feel is really worth the effort. You can mince the chicken in a food processor if you have one. Serve the croquettes as a first course or offer them as a main course! With new potatoes and some fresh green asparagus they will be quite luxurious.

450 g/1 lb minced chicken
2 eggs, beaten
50 g/2 oz fresh breadcrumbs
1 tablespoon chopped fresh
  tarragon
1 tablespoon chopped chives
2 tablespoons dry sherry
4 tablespoons double cream
salt and freshly ground black
  pepper

100 g/4 oz slightly stale bread
flour for coating
1 quantity Bearnaise Sauce to
  serve (page 169)
oil for deep frying
Garnish
sprigs of tarragon
slices of lemon

Mix the chicken with one of the eggs, the breadcrumbs, herbs, sherry and cream. Add seasoning to taste and beat the meat well to make sure that it is well combined. Chill thoroughly for 1 hour.

Make fine breadcrumbs from the stale bread, using a liquidiser or food processor or rubbing it on a grater. Put them on a large plate and prepare a second plate with some flour and a little seasoning, well mixed in. Have the remaining beaten egg ready in a shallow dish.

Roughly divide the chicken mixture into eight portions. Put each one in turn in the flour, coat it thoroughly, place it on a clean work surface and shape it into a cylindrical croquette. Lift each croquette into the beaten egg with the palette knife, brush egg all over it and then lift it in to the breadcrumbs, sprinkling them generously over the top and pressing them well on to the sides. Brush off any excess then put the croquette back on the work surface and neaten it again by patting the top and sides with the palette knife. When you are satisfied that the croquettes are as neat as possible, put them on a baking tray lined with cling film and chill in either the freezer or freezing compartment of the refrigerator for about 45 minutes before cooking them or leave them in the refrigerator for several hours so that the coating is well hardened.

Make the Bearnaise sauce according to the recipe instructions. Heat the oil for deep frying to 180 C/350 F. Cook the croquettes until golden. Drain on absorbent kitchen paper and keep the cooked croquettes hot while the remainder are being fried. Arrange them on a serving dish, add the garnish and serve the sauce separately. **Serves 4**

Chicken Swirls

(Illustrated on page 168)

This is an economical yet impressive dish to serve at a dinner party. As with most pasta dishes, a green salad is an ideal accompaniment for these chicken rolls.

$\frac{1}{2}$ quantity pasta dough (see
    Ravioli, page 138)
450 g/1 lb minced chicken
50 g/2 oz fresh breadcrumbs
2 eggs, beaten
salt and freshly ground black
    pepper
2 tablespoons chopped fresh
    basil or 2 teaspoons dried
    basil

1 chicken stock cube
300 ml/$\frac{3}{4}$ pint boiling water
4 tablespoons concentrated
    tomato purée
about 300 ml/$\frac{1}{2}$ pint full-bodied
    red wine
garlic salt
50 g/2 oz Gruyère cheese, grated

Make the pasta dough following the recipe instructions for Ravioli and roll it out into a rectangle measuring about 25 × 42 cm/10 × 17 in.

Mix the chicken with the breadcrumbs, one egg, seasoning and basil. Brush the pasta all over with some of the remaining beaten egg, then spread the chicken mixture over it, leaving a border all the way round. Roll up from the long end, brushing more egg over the pasta as you roll it up. Make sure the end is well brushed with beaten egg and press it down firmly. Trim off the very ends of the roll, then use a sharp serrated knife to cut the rest into 16 slices.

Bring a large saucepan of salted water to the boil and add a little oil. Cook the pasta swirls by lowering them gently into the water. Bring back to the boil and boil for 1 minute. Use a draining spoon to lift the swirls from the water, then put them into a large ovenproof dish. You will probably have to cook the swirls in two or three batches but this is still very quick.

Dissolve the stock cube in the boiling water then stir in the tomato purée and enough wine to make 600 ml/1 pint. Add a little garlic salt and pour the liquid over the swirls. Cover with cooking foil and bake in a moderate oven (180 C, 350 F, gas 4) for 1 hour.

Sprinkle the cheese over the swirls and cook under a hot grill until golden. Serve at once. **Serves 4**

Chicken Timbales Tonnato

(Illustrated on page 168)

Serve two of these small chicken timbales per person, arranging them attractively on individual plates. Lightly cooked vegetables – broccoli, mange-tout peas, French beans or courgettes and potatoes – would make the ideal accompaniment. For a starter, halve the quantities of chicken mixture and offer one timbale for each person, with some crisp melba toast.

675 g/1½ lb minced chicken
75 g/3 oz fresh white
   breadcrumbs
1 egg, beaten
salt and freshly ground black
   pepper
grated rind of 1 small lemon
2 tablespoons double cream
a little butter

Sauce
1 (198-g/7-oz) can tuna in oil
1 clove garlic, peeled and
   crushed
juice of ½ lemon
150 ml/¼ pint mayonnaise
Garnish
2 (5-cm/2-in) lengths cucumber
4 twists of lemon

Mix the chicken with the breadcrumbs, egg, seasoning to taste and the lemon rind. Stir in the cream. Line the bases of eight ramekin dishes with greaseproof paper and make sure they are well greased. Divide the chicken mixture between the dishes and dot the top of each with a little butter. Put a small piece of greaseproof paper on top of each, stand the ramekins in a roasting tin and pour in boiling water to come halfway up the sides of the outer tin. Bake in a moderate oven (180 C, 350 F, gas 4) for 45 minutes.

For the sauce, mash the tuna with the oil from the can, the garlic and the lemon juice, or, blend in a liquidiser or food processor. Stir in the mayonnaise and add seasoning to taste. Chill for at least 30 minutes.

For the garnish, cut the pieces of cucumber in half lengthways, then cut each piece into long thin slices, leaving them all attached at one end. Place the pieces of cucumber in ice-cold water to open out.

Turn out the cooked timbales and remove the greaseproof paper. Put two on each plate and add a piece of cucumber to each portion, opening out the slices like a fan. Add a twist of lemon and serve, handing the sauce separately. **Serves 4**

Turkey Roll en Croute

1 kg/2 lb minced turkey
100 g/4 oz fresh breadcrumbs
salt and freshly ground black
  pepper
1 egg, beaten

1 quantity Cream cheese with
  Garlic and Herbs (page 171)
1 (397-g/13-oz) packet frozen
  puff pastry, thawed
beaten egg to glaze

Mix the turkey with the breadcrumbs and seasoning then mix in the beaten egg. Prepare and chill the cream cheese roll according to the recipe instructions and shape the turkey mixture evenly around it to enclose it completely, including the ends. Chill while you roll out the pastry.

On a lightly floured surface, roll out the pastry into an oblong shape large enough to enclose the turkey roll with about 5 cm/2 in to spare down one long side. Put the turkey roll on the pastry, fold one side over and brush the edge with a little beaten egg. Fold the opposite side over and trim off the excess, then press the join to seal it well. Fold the ends over to enclose the filling completely, brushing the pastry with beaten egg where necessary and trimming off any excess. Turn the roll over so that the seam is underneath and lay it on a baking tray.

Re-roll the pastry trimmings and cut out as many leaves as you can, brush them with beaten egg and press them on the roll in a herringbone pattern. Glaze the pastry with beaten egg then bake in a moderately hot oven (200 C, 400 F, gas 6) for 1 hour, or until well puffed and golden brown. Serve immediately. **Serves 4 to 6**

Steak Tartare

This is a traditional French recipe for only the very finest of minced steak, minced at the latest possible stage before serving.

450 g/1 lb freshly minced fillet
  steak
1 tablespoon chopped capers
dash of Worcestershire sauce
salt and freshly ground black
  pepper

2 tablespoons chopped parsley
4 egg yolks
4 tablespoon finely chopped
  onion
4 tablespoon finely chopped
  green pepper

It is essential that the fillet steak is perfectly fresh. Mix it with the capers, Worcestershire sauce, a little seasoning and parsley, then divide it into four equal portions. Place one portion of meat on each of four plates, mounding it hamburger style. Make a small hollow in each portion of meat and put an egg yolk into it. Offer the remaining ingredients separately, in tiny bowls. **Serves 4**

Fritter Salad

(Illustrated on pages 166/167)

Hot beef and chick pea fritters blend with fresh crisp ingredients in an unusual salad which can be served with some hot crusty bread to make a light meal or with baked potatoes for a more substantial menu.

450 g/1 lb minced beef
1 small onion, peeled and finely chopped
1 clove garlic, peeled and crushed
grated rind and juice of 1 lemon
$\frac{1}{2}$ teaspoon chopped thyme
2 tablespoons chopped parsley
1 (383-g/13$\frac{1}{2}$-oz) can chick peas, drained
salt and freshly ground black pepper
Batter
100 g/4 oz plain flour
2 eggs
several drops of sesame oil
150 ml/$\frac{1}{4}$ pint milk
Salad
1 small Chinese cabbage

1 bunch spring onions
$\frac{1}{2}$ cucumber
4 tomatoes
8–10 black olives, stoned
2 tablespoons sesame seeds, lightly toasted
Yogurt dressing
2 tablespoons chopped fresh mint
1 teaspoon sugar
150 ml/$\frac{1}{4}$ pint natural yogurt
Peanut dressing
2 tablespoons smooth peanut butter
4 tablespoons lemon juice
4 tablespoons mayonnaise
$\frac{1}{2}$ teaspoon chilli powder
oil for deep frying

First make the beef and chick pea balls: mix the meat with the onion, garlic, lemon rind and juice, thyme and parsley and mash the chick peas – they do not have to be smooth but they should be quite well broken down. Add them to the mince, mix in seasoning to taste and make sure all the ingredients are well combined. Dampen your hands and shape the mixture into 24 small meatballs. Chill these for at least 30 minutes.

For the batter, sift the flour into a bowl and add a generous pinch of salt then make a well in the centre. Break the eggs into the well, sprinkle in the sesame oil and then gradually beat in the milk, incorporating the flour little by little to make a smooth batter. Beat thoroughly and set aside while you prepare the salad.

Shred the Chinese cabbage; trim and shred the spring onions into long fine strips. Lightly peel the cucumber, then cut it in half lengthways and cut each half into 5-cm/2-in lengths. Slice these into thin strips. Peel the tomatoes (see page 144) and roughly chop them. Roughly chop the olives. Toss all the salad ingredients together in a bowl, sprinkling in the sesame seeds, then transfer the salad to a large serving platter or bowl, making a slight well in the middle of the ingredients ready for the fritters.

Before cooking the fritters prepare the dressings. For the yogurt dressing, mix the mint with the sugar, crushing the grains with the back of a teaspoon, stir in the yogurt and seasoning to taste, then transfer to a serving dish and chill. Mix all the ingredients for the peanut dressing, adding seasoning to taste. Put in a serving bowl and set aside.

Heat the oil for deep frying to 180 C/350 F or until a cube of bread browns in 30 seconds. Give the batter a quick whisk then dip the meatballs into it and fry them in the hot oil a few at a time until crisp and golden. Drain on absorbent kitchen paper and then pile the fritters in the middle of the salad. Serve at once, tossing the fritters lightly into the salad at the table, and serving the mixture on to individual plates. Offer the dressings separately. **Serves 4**

Minced Veal Cordon Bleu

(Illustrated on pages 166/167)

Minced veal is considerably cheaper than escalopes and this recipe presents the mince in a way that makes it seem just as special.

450 g/1 lb minced veal
50 g/2 oz fresh breadcrumbs
salt and freshly ground black
  pepper
2 tablespoons chopped chives
4 slices Emmental cheese
4 slices Parma ham (or use
  cooked ham if you prefer)
flour for coating
1 large egg, beaten

100 g/4 oz fine white
  breadcrumbs
50 g/2 oz butter
2 tablespoons oil
1 quantity White Wine Sauce
  (page 164) to serve
Garnish
1 lemon, sliced
flat-leafed parsley sprigs

Mix the veal with the fresh breadcrumbs and seasoning, add the chives and make sure the ingredients are thoroughly combined. Divide the meat into four equal portions. Shape each portion of meat into a fairly thin oval cake, lay a slice of cheese on top and wrap the ham carefully around the meat and cheese, keeping the oval shape as neat as possible and trimming off any tiny corners of cheese as appropriate. Coat each cake in flour, then in beaten egg and then thoroughly in the breadcrumbs. Repeat the process a second time then chill the cakes thoroughly until the coating is hardened.

Melt the butter with the oil in a large frying pan. When hot add the cakes and cook over a moderate heat until golden underneath, then turn and cook the other side. Drain on absorbent kitchen paper and serve at once, garnished with the lemon slices and parsley. Hand the sauce separately. **Serves 4**

Celeriac Circles

(Illustrated on page 165)

Celeriac is a root vegetable with the same flavour as celery. Here it is topped with a minced pork mixture and served with a pale green broccoli sauce. Serve new potatoes or sauté potatoes with the main dish and prepare some carrots as another accompaniment if you like.

1 large celeriac root
salt and freshly ground black
  pepper
450 g/1 lb minced beef
25 g/1 oz fresh breadcrumbs
1 egg, beaten
1 tablespoon made mustard (use
  a fairly mild one, for example
  Dijon mustard)

225 g/8 oz broccoli
1 quantity White Wine Sauce
  (page 164)
Garnish
8 rindless rashers bacon
1 small tomato, quartered

Peel the celeriac, then cut four 2.5-cm/1-in thick slices from it (do not cut them from the very ends or they will not be large enough). Cook these in simmering salted water for 15 minutes, then drain.

Mix the beef with the breadcrumbs, egg, mustard and seasoning to taste, then divide it into four equal portions. Press the meat on to the celeriac circles, moulding it neatly into four cakes. Place these on a thoroughly greased baking tray and cook in a moderately hot oven (200 C, 400 F, gas 6) for 45 minutes.

Meanwhile, trim and cook the broccoli in boiling salted water for 15 minutes or until tender. If the stalks are small and young 5 to 10 minutes cooking time may be adequate. Drain thoroughly. Make the white wine sauce according to the recipe instructions, then blend in a liquidiser or food processor with the cooked broccoli. Pour this sauce back into the saucepan, adjust the seasoning as necessary and heat very gently.

For the garnish, roll the bacon rashers up and thread them on to one or two metal skewers. Cook them under a hot grill until golden. Thread two bacon rolls on either side of a tomato quarter on each of four wooden cocktail sticks.

Arrange the celeriac circles on individual plates or one large serving platter and pour a little of the sauce over each one. Top each circle with one of the cocktail stick garnishes and serve immediately, handing the remaining sauce separately. **Serves 4**

Beef and Spinach Rolls

This is an unusual casserole-type dish which is good on a cold day. Serve with plenty of buttered pasta, rice and vegetables or a salad.

675 g/1½ lb minced beef
100 g/4 oz fresh breadcrumbs
1 egg, beaten
1 (227-g/8-oz) packet frozen
   spinach, thawed and
   thoroughly drained
freshly grated nutmeg
salt and freshly ground black
   pepper
100 g/4 oz rindless streaky
   bacon, chopped
oil for cooking

1 large onion, peeled and
   chopped
3 tablespoons plain flour
1 beef stock cube
150 ml/¼ pint boiling water
450 ml/¾ pint Guiness
2 tablespoons concentrated
   tomato purée
225 g/8 oz button mushrooms,
   sliced
150 ml/¼ pint soured cream
2 tablespoons chopped parsley

Mix the beef with the breadcrumbs, egg, spinach and a generous sprinkling of nutmeg. Stir in seasoning to taste and mix thoroughly. Divide the mixture into eight equal portions then shape each into a 7.5-cm/3-in long roll. Chill for at least 1 hour.

Dry fry the bacon in a large frying pan until it is crisp and brown then remove it from the pan, leaving all the fat behind. Drain on absorbent kitchen paper and set aside for garnish. Add a little extra oil to the pan if necessary, then brown the rolls all over, keeping them neat, and remove them from the pan. Drain on absorbent kitchen paper and set aside.

Add the onion to the pan and cook until soft but not brown. Stir in the flour and cook for a minute. Dissolve the stock cube in the boiling water then pour it into the pan and stir in the Guinness. Add the tomato purée and bring to the boil. Return the rolls to the pan and simmer gently for 30 minutes. About 5 minutes before the end of the cooking time add the mushrooms to the sauce.

To serve, arrange the rolls on a serving dish and pour the sauce over. Pour the soured cream down the middle of the rolls and sprinkle the crunchy bacon on top. Garnish with parsley and serve immediately.
Serves 4

Ham and Beef Rolls

(Illustrated on pages 166/167)

This is an economical but interesting casserole. Offer buttered noodles or creamed potatoes with it.

450 g/1 lb minced beef
1 tablespoon horseradish sauce
salt and freshly ground black
    pepper
2 tablespoons chopped parsley
4 slices cooked ham
1 large onion, peeled and
    chopped

50 g/2 oz butter
100 g/4 oz walnut halves
2 tablespoons plain flour
1 beef stock cube
300 ml/$\frac{1}{2}$ pint red wine
150 ml/$\frac{1}{4}$ pint water
25 g/1 oz raisins

Mix the beef with the horseradish sauce and seasoning to taste. Add the parsley and make sure all the ingredients are thoroughly combined. Divide the mixture into four equal portions and spread one over each slice of ham. Roll up neatly, then place the ham rolls in an ovenproof dish.

Fry the onion in the butter until soft but not browned. Add the walnuts and cook for a few minutes, then stir in the flour and crumble in the stock cube. Pour in the wine and water then add the raisins. Bring to the boil, then pour this sauce over the ham and cover the dish with cooking foil. Bake in a moderately hot oven (200 C, 400 F, gas 6) for 45 minutes. Serve piping hot. **Serves 4**

Fennel-stuffed Pork

A simple stuffing of chopped fennel, breadcrumbs and cream cheese makes an excellent addition to this otherwise plain pork meat loaf. Served with a wine sauce, buttered noodles and courgettes or carrots this recipe will grace any dinner table.

450 g/1 lb minced pork
175 g/6 oz fresh white
    breadcrumbs
salt and freshly ground black
    pepper
1 egg, beaten
2 large onions, peeled and finely
    chopped

2 heads fennel, trimmed and
    finely chopped
225 g/8 oz cream cheese
1 quantity White Wine Sauce
    (page 164) to serve

Mix the pork with 50 g/2 oz of the breadcrumbs, seasoning to taste and the egg. Add half the chopped onion and mix thoroughly.

Line the base of a 1-kg/2-lb loaf tin with greaseproof paper then grease the tin thoroughly. Press three-quarters of the meat mixture round the inside of the tin. Mix the remaining breadcrumbs with the remaining onion, fennel and cream cheese. Add seasoning to taste and press this mixture into the middle of the loaf tin. Cover the top with the remaining meat mixture.

Cover the tin with cooking foil and bake in a moderate oven (180 C, 350 F, gas 4) for 1 hour. Turn the cooked loaf out on to a serving platter and serve the sauce separately. **Serves 4**

Stuffed Fennel

Braised, meat-filled fennel makes an interesting main dish. Serve new potatoes or sautéed potatoes and a simple vegetable dish with the fennel. French beans, courgettes or mange-tout peas would all go quite well.

450 g/1 lb minced steak
1 clove garlic, peeled and
   crushed
1 small onion, peeled and grated
2 tablespoons concentrated
   tomato purée
salt and freshly ground black
   pepper
1 teaspoon marjoram

4 bulbs fennel (each about
   9–10 oz/250–275 g in weight)
2 tablespoons olive oil
1 chicken stock cube
2 tablespoons plain flour
300 ml/$\frac{1}{2}$ pint water
150 ml/$\frac{1}{4}$ pint single cream
dash of lemon juice

Mix the minced steak with the garlic, onion and tomato purée. Stir in seasoning to taste and the marjoram.

Cut just the top off each bulb of fennel, then carefully remove all the middle part. To do this use a small pointed knife and make lots of criss-cross cuts down into the vegetable, then gradually remove the inside, leaving a neat shell.

Stuff the prepared meat mixture into the fennel shells and stand them in a greased ovenproof dish.

Finely chop the scooped-out fennel (or use a food processor if you have one). Heat the oil in a frying pan or saucepan then add the fennel and fry over a medium heat until the pieces are just beginning to brown. Stir in the stock cube and flour and cook for a minute, then pour in the water and bring to the boil, stirring all the ime. Pour this mixture round the stuffed fennel, then cover the dish and bake in a moderate oven (180 C, 350 F, gas 4) for 1 hour or until the bulbs of fennel are tender.

Carefully stir the cream into the sauce and add just a little lemon juice, then return the dish to the oven for 4 to 5 minutes before serving. **Serves 4**

SAUCES AND SIDE DISHES

Throughout the chapters, many of the recipes include suggestions for side dishes which will complement them or to complete the meal. In come cases this is because the dish itself is slightly unusual but often it may be to ring the changes on a traditional menu theme or to remind you of the old favourites, like a simple green salad. In addition, you will find that some dishes require recipes from this chapter as an essential ingredient. So have a look through these last few pages, you may find that they inspire you to adapt or even extend the ideas offered in the main part of the book.

Béchamel Sauce

600 ml/1 pint milk	2 cloves
bay leaf	50 g/2 oz butter
blade of mace	50 g/2 oz plain flour
4 black peppercorns	salt

Pour the milk into a saucepan, add the bay leaf and mace, stir in the peppercorns and cloves then heat slowly to boiling point. Remove the pan from the heat and allow the milk to cool. When cold strain the milk to remove the flavouring ingredients.

Melt the butter in a saucepan and add the flour, stirring all the time. Cook for 1 minute before pouring in the milk – do this gradually while stirring continuously. Bring to the boil and cook for 2 minutes, then add salt and use as required. **Makes 600 ml/1 pint**

Cheese Sauce
Add 100 g/4 oz grated Cheddar cheese to the sauce. Stir in 1 tablespoon prepared mustard to give extra bite.

Mushroom Sauce
Sauté 100 g/4 oz sliced button mushrooms in the butter before stirring in the flour. Continue as in the main recipe. A little paprika is good in mushroom sauce.

Onion Sauce
Finely chop 225 g/8 oz onions and thoroughly fry them in the butter before adding the flour. Do not let the onions brown. Continue as above, simmering the sauce for 5 minutes once all the milk has been added.

Mustard Sauce
Use mustard powder instead of the flour in the main recipe.

Tomato Sauce

50 g/2 oz butter
1 large onion, peeled and
    chopped
bay leaf
1 clove garlic, peeled and
    crushed
1 chicken stock cube
2 (397-g/14-oz) cans chopped
    tomatoes

2 tablespoons concentrated
    tomato purée
300 ml/½ pint boiling water
sprig of thyme
salt and freshly ground black
    pepper

Melt the butter in a saucepan then add the onion, bay leaf and garlic
and cook until the onion is soft but not browned. Crumble in the stock
cube, pour in the tomatoes and stir in the purée. Pour in the the water,
add the thyme and bring to the boil. Cover the pan and reduce the heat
so that the sauce simmers, then cook for 45 minutes.

Remove the bay leaf and thyme and blend the sauce in a liquidiser or
food processor until smooth. Pour back into the pan, taste and adjust
the seasoning, then reheat and serve. **Makes about 600 ml/1 pint**

Rich Tomato Sauce
Substitute red wine for the water in the above recipe.

Tomato and Celery Sauce
Wash and finely chop 1 small head of celery and fry it with the onion.
Continue as above.

Barbecue Sauce

2 tablespoons oil
1 large onion, peeled and
    chopped
2 cloves garlic, peeled and
    crushed
2 tablespoons plain flour
2 tablespoons made mustard
2 tablespoons soy sauce

2 tablespoons soft brown sugar
1 tablespoon red wine vinegar
6 tablespoons concentrated
    tomato purée
1 beef stock cube
300 ml/½ pint water
salt and freshly ground black
    pepper

Heat the oil in a saucepan and cook the onion and garlic until the onion
is soft but not browned. Stir in the flour and mustard, then the soy
sauce, sugar and vinegar. Add the tomato purée and crumble in the
stock cube before pouring in the water. Bring to the boil and simmer for
5 minutes then blend the sauce until smooth in a liquidiser or food
processor. Taste and adjust the seasoning then reheat the sauce before
serving. **Makes 450 ml/¾ pint**

Red Wine Sauce

50 g/2 oz butter
1 large onion, peeled and
  chopped
1 clove garlic, peeled and
  crushed
bay leaf
1 teaspoon chopped thyme
50 g/2 oz plain flour
1 chicken stock cube

600 ml/1 pint full-bodied red
  wine
2 tablespoons concentrated
  tomato purée
salt and freshly ground black
  pepper
100 g/4 oz button mushrooms,
  sliced (optional)

Melt the butter in a saucepan and cook the onion with the garlic until
the onion is soft but not browned. Add the bay leaf and thyme then stir
in the flour. Crumble in the stock cube and pour in the wine. Stir in the
tomato purée, add seasoning to taste and bring to the boil. Simmer for 5
minutes, stir in the mushrooms if used, then cook for a further 2
minutes before using as required. **Makes 600 ml/1 pint**

White Wine Sauce

50 g/2 oz butter
1 large onion, peeled and
  chopped
bay leaf
1 chicken stock cube
50 g/2 oz plain flour

450 ml/$\frac{3}{4}$ pint dry white wine
salt and freshly ground black
  pepper
100 g/4 oz button mushrooms,
  sliced (optional)
150 ml/$\frac{1}{4}$ pint single cream

Melt the butter in a saucepan and cook the onion until soft but not
browned. Add the bay leaf, crumble in the stock cube and stir in the
flour. Pour in the wine, add seasoning to taste, and bring to the boil.
Reduce the heat and simmer for 5 minutes. Add the mushrooms, if used,
then simmer for a further 2 minutes. Finally stir in the cream and heat
gently without boiling. Use as required. **Makes 600 ml/1 pint**

Opposite page *Top: Chicken Croquettes (page 152); Below: Celeriac
Circles (page 158)* **Overleaf** *Clockwise from bottom right: Ham and
Beef Rolls (page 160), Minced Veal Cordon Bleu (page 157) and
Fritter Salad (page 156)*

Sweet and Sour Sauce

1 green pepper
2 tablespoons oil
a few drops of sesame oil
1 large onion, peeled and
  roughly chopped
1 large carrot, cut into strips
1 tablespoon cornflour

2 tablespoons water
2 tablespoons soy sauce
3 tablespoons tomato ketchup
1 tablespoon red wine vinegar
1 (340-g/12-oz) can pineapple
  pieces in syrup
2 tablespoons dry sherry

Cut the stalk end off the pepper and remove all the pith and seeds from inside. Cut the flesh into chunks. Heat the oil with the sesame oil in a saucepan, add the onion, pepper and carrot and fry quickly for 2 to 3 minutes. The vegetables should be slightly crisp.

Blend the cornflour with the water then stir in all the remaining ingredients. Pour this mixture into the saucepan and bring to the boil. Simmer, stirring, for 2 minutes, then serve at once. **Makes about 450 ml/¾ pint**

Béarnaise Sauce

4 tablespoons distilled white
  vinegar
bay leaf
4 black peppercorns

blade of mace
sprig of tarragon
2 egg yolks
100 g/4 oz butter

Pour the vinegar into a saucepan and add the bay leaf, peppercorns, mace and tarragon. Bring to the boil then boil steadily until the liquid has reduced by just over half.

Put the egg yolks in a heatproof basin. Add a small knob of the butter and put the bowl over a saucepan of just simmering water. Whisking continuously, add the strained vinegar. Gradually whisk in the butter, knob by knob, until it melts and the sauce has thickened. Pour the sauce into a warmed sauceboat and serve at once. **Serves 4**

Top: Chicken Timbales Tonnato (page 154); Below: Chicken Swirls (page 153)

Mayonnaise

2 egg yolks (at room temperature)
salt and freshly ground black pepper
1 teaspoon mustard powder

½ teaspoon caster sugar
3 tablespoons lemon juice
250 ml/8 fl oz corn oil or olive oil

Put the egg yolks in a basin and leave them until they are warmed to room temperature. Add a generous sprinkling of seasoning, the mustard, sugar and lemon juice. Add just a few drops of oil and whisk the mixture thoroughly until the eggs become pale. Continue whisking vigorously, adding the oil drop by drop. Gradually the mixture will become pale and thick. If you have an electric blender or food mixer that is the best piece of equipment to use for this (see below). Chill the mayonnaise before use. **Makes about 300 ml/½ pint**

To Rescue Curdled Mayonnaise
If the mayonnaise does curdle, all is not lost. Take a perfectly clean bowl, break two egg yolks into it and add just a little of the curdled mixture (about 1 tablespoon). Whisk very thoroughly indeed, then gradually start adding the curdled mixture little by little. It is important to whisk quite vigorously.

Liquidiser Mayonnaise
The mayonnaise can be made most successfully in a blender or liquidiser, adding the oil drop by drop by drop through the special opening in the top cover as the machine runs.

Flavoured Mayonnaises
Garlic Mayonnaise Add 1 crushed clove of garlic to the prepared mayonnaise.
Lemon Mayonnaise. Add the grated rind of ½ lemon to the prepared mayonnaise.
Herb Mayonnaise. Add 4 tablespoons chopped fresh herbs to the prepared mayonnaise. Chopped parsley, thyme, marjoram, rosemary, tarragon, chives or any other fresh herbs can be either combined or used individually.
Pink Mayonnaise. Add 2 tablespoons concentrated tomato purée and 1 tablespoon lemon juice to the mayonnaise. A crushed clove of garlic also goes well if you like.
Green Sauce. Blend 1 trimmed bunch of watercress to a purée with 2 tablespoons double cream, then stir it into the mayonnaise.
Devilled Mayonnaise. Add 1 tablespoon concentrated tomato purée, 1 tablespoon strong prepared mustard, a generous dash of Worcestershire sauce and 1 crushed clove garlic to the mayonnaise.
Horseradish Mayonnaise. Add 2 to 4 tablespoons horseradish sauce to the mayonnaise.

Mustard Mayonnaise. Add 2 to 4 tablespoons prepared mustard of your choice to the mayonnaise.

Sweet and Sour Mayonnaise. Add 4 tablespoons bottled sweet and sour sauce to the mayonnaise.

Anchovy Mayonnaise. Mash 1 (50-g/2-oz) can anchovies with their oil, then add 2 tablespoons lemon juice and the grated rind of 1 lemon. Mix the anchovy paste into the mayonnaise, taste and add a little extra lemon juice if necessary.

Flavoured Butters

These are good with freshly cooked burgers, to fry various ingredients or to flavour a simple sauce. Add the ingredients to the butter and beat well, then form the butter into a roll, wrap it in cling film and chill until firm. Slice to serve. The following quantities will flavour 100 g/4 oz butter.

Garlic Butter. Add 1 large clove garlic, crushed.

Herb Butter. Add 4 tablespoons chopped fresh herbs.

Lemon Butter. Add the grated rind of 1 lemon and 2 tablespoons lemon juice.

Anchovy Butter. Thoroughly mash 1 (50-g/2-oz) can anchovy fillets with their oil. Beat them into the butter with a dash of lemon juice.

Nut Butter. Grind 100 g/4 oz roasted peanuts to a powder and beat them into the butter.

Note. You can combine some of the above ideas, for example herbs can be mixed with garlic, lemon can be mixed with either garlic or herbs and garlic and herbs can be mixed with anchovies.

Cream Cheese Toppings

Beat any of the following flavourings into 225 g/8 oz cream cheese and chill thoroughly in the shape of a roll. Serve sliced on top of plain hamburgers or as required.

Cream Cheese with Garlic and Herbs. Add 1 clove garlic, crushed and 4 tablespoons chopped fresh herbs.

Lemon and Parsley Cheese. Add the grated rind of 1 lemon and 4 tablespoons chopped fresh parsley to the cheese.

Walnut and Caper Cheese. Add 100 g/4 oz finely chopped walnuts and 2 tablespoons chopped capers to the cheese.

Sesame Cream Cheese. Add 4 tablespoons ground sesame seeds to the cheese.

Cheese with Pineapple and Chives. Drain 1 (340-g/12-oz) can of pineapple pieces and chop the fruit. Mix 2 tablespoons chives and the fruit into the cream cheese. Chill, then spoon the mixture over hamburgers rather than shaping and slicing it.

Making a Green Salad

Telling people how to make a green salad may seem pedantic and unnecessary, but there's a good reason for it – there are good green salads and awful limp efforts that bear more resemblance to the additions to a compost heap than they do to salad! At its simplest, a green salad can be good, fresh crisp lettuce dressed with some chopped herbs, oil and a little lemon juice, but I prefer to mix lots of ingredients – celery, chicory, iceberg or cos lettuce, Chinese leaves, spring onions, courgettes, cucumber, green pepper and avocado pear. So that the flavours mingle and complement each other, shred or slice the ingredients finely. The purists would say lettuce should be torn with your hands but personally I always use a knife.

Once you've chosen and cut up the ingredients, put those that should be very crisp – lettuce, celery, cucumber, spring onions and courgettes – in a bowl of iced water and leave them there for at least 30 minutes. If you are adding avocados, leave their preparation until just before you toss the salad together or they may discolour. Drain the ingredients thoroughly and whizz them round in a salad spinner to remove the last of the water, then mix them all together in a bowl – make it large so that you can toss the dressing in.

For the dressing use olive oil – about 4 to 6 tablespoons – and either lemon juice or wine vinegar, using half the quantity of lemon juice or vinegar to oil. Add mustard, salt and freshly ground black pepper, a little sugar, crushed garlic and chopped parsley, tasting the dressing as you go along to get it just right. If you are using avocados, cut them in half, remove the stones and slice the peeled flesh. Toss all the ingredients together, adding dressing to taste, and serve at once.

Tomato and Mozzarella Salad

450 g/1 lb tomatoes, peeled (page 144) and sliced
225 g/8 oz mozzarrella cheese, sliced
1 small onion, peeled and finely chopped
2 tablespoons chopped parsley

4 tablespoons olive oil
2 tablespoons lemon juice
1 clove garlic, peeled and crushed
salt and freshly ground black pepper

Arrange the tomatoes and cheese on a large serving plate and sprinkle the onion and parsley evenly over the top.

Put the oil, lemon juice and garlic with the seasoning, in a screw-topped jar, and shake well. Pour this dressing over the salad and serve at once. **Serves 4 to 6**

Spinach and Bacon Salad

450 g/1 lb fresh young spinach,
    trimmed and thoroughly
    washed
225 g/8 oz lean rindless bacon,
    chopped
1 bunch spring onions, chopped
4 tablespoons olive oil

2 tablespoons lemon juice
1 clove garlic, peeled and
    crushed
1 tablespoon made mustard
salt and freshly ground black
    pepper

Make sure the spinach is thoroughly drained then shred it finely. Dry
fry the bacon until crisp. Drain on absorbent kitchen paper and set
aside to cool.

Put the spinach in a salad bowl and mix in the spring onions, then
add the cooled bacon. Mix all the remaining ingredients in a screw-top
jar and shake thoroughly. Pour this dressing over the salad just before
serving and toss well. **Serves 4 to 6**

Avocado and Orange Salad

2 large ripe avocado pears
juice of 1 lemon
2 oranges
1 small iceberg lettuce, shredded
1 small onion, peeled and cut
    into fine slices

4 tablespoons olive oil
salt and freshly ground black
    pepper

Halve the pears and remove their stones then peel and slice the flesh.
Put the slices in a basin and sprinkle the lemon juice on top.

Grate the rind from 1 orange and sprinkle it on to the avocado slices.
Peel the oranges, removing all the pith, then cut between the
membranes and remove each segment separately. Put the orange
segments into a salad bowl. Add the lettuce, drained avocado and the
onion slices, separated into rings. Sprinkle the olive oil over the salad
and add seasoning to taste. Toss well and serve at once. **Serves 4**

Greek Salad

225 g/8 oz tomatoes, peeled
  (page 144) and quartered
1 small onion, peeled and thinly
  sliced
225 g/8 oz feta cheese, cubed
¼ cucumber, lightly peeled and
  cut into cubes

100 g/4 oz black olives, stoned
1 small lettuce heart, shredded
4 tablespoons olive oil
1 clove garlic, peeled and
  crushed (optional)
salt and freshly ground black
  pepper

Mix all the ingredients together in a large bowl and toss lightly. Serve
lightly chilled. **Serves 4**

Caesar Salad

1 crisp lettuce, for example
  iceberg or cos, shredded
4 spring onions, chopped
1 (50-g/2-oz) can anchovy
  fillets, drained and chopped
4 slices white bread
6 tablespoons olive oil

1 clove garlic, peeled and
  crushed
salt and freshly ground black
  pepper
1 egg yolk
4 tablespoons lemon juice
1 tablespoon made mustard

Put the lettuce, spring onions and anchovies in a salad bowl and toss
well. Cut the bread into small cubes, then fry these in 4 tablespoons of
the oil with the garlic added until crisp and golden on all sides. Drain
the croûtons and add to the salad.

Whisk the seasoning and egg yolk with the lemon juice and mustard,
then whisk in the remaining oil and pour the dressing over the salad.
Toss well, then serve at once. *Serves 4 to 6*

Note. Traditionally a whole egg should be used in the salad dressing but
using the yolk alone gives a less pronounced flavour.